Alcoholic Doctor

Dr Anish Kumar Kurar

London | New York

Published by Clink Street Publishing 2019

Copyright © 2019

First edition.

The author asserts the moral right under the Copyright, Designs and Patents Act 1988 to be identified as the author of this work.

All rights reserved. No part of this publication may be reproduced, stored in a retrieval system or transmitted, in any form or by any means without the prior consent of the author, nor be otherwise circulated in any form of binding or cover other than that with which it is published and without a similar condition being imposed on the subsequent purchaser.

ISBN:
978-1-912850-62-4 paperback
978-1-912850-63-1 ebook

Dr ANISH KUMAR KURAR

True Life Story

Born - 3rd May 1950

Delhi India

Dr Anish Kumar Kurar

Alcoholic Doctor

1st Class 1st – Delhi University B.Sc. 1969
FRCS Royal College of Edinburgh, UK, 1986
Retired Senior Consultant – Orthopaedics

Saudi Arabia	2001
United Kingdom	2008
India	2010

Acclaimed in newspapers a number of times for his medical achievements.

My eldest brother told me:
"So many people have achieved in this world, but the way you achieved is very unique."
My elder brother told me:
"Who learns to live alone can do anything in his life."
For me, I knew from the beginning my God and I would do the job and we did it.

Special thank you to:

Dr Kuldip Kashyap
Friend and General Practitioner, London

Jueta Kurar
My Daughter
Banker, London

Langhit Kurar
Dr/Mr – My Son
Fellow of the Royal College of Surgeons – Orthopaedics, London

Ishaan Hemnani
Son-in-law
Engineer, London
For their assistance with my book

I started my life journey from the age of nine months, when I became aware of my existence on this beautiful planet, our good Earth.

I was told in my childhood that what you sow is what you reap. I am approaching seventy years of my life. I am a retired Senior Orthopaedic Consultant. My family is middle class and I have three elder sisters and two elder brothers, myself to arrive last, and my great father and mother.

My enjoyment of retirement comes from my memories of deeds that I did in my life as advised by God.

My memories of my life go back to less than one year into my life, when I became aware of my existence: Myself in my father's lap with my mother by his side, and standing outside the well-lit decorated hall on the occasion of the wedding of my eldest sister. I remember this because I was in my father's lap wearing a fur coat of real tiger skin, yellow in colour with black spots. I liked this so much and my mother tried to stop me so many times but I could not resist chewing on the soft fur.

When I was three years old, my second sister got married. I remember only because the marriage was in summer. Indian summers, with so many mangoes available. I still remember they were there in a big tub full of water and lots of ice. Because the family members were busy with their marriage, I with my cousins, we stole so many mangoes and thoroughly enjoyed them.

The favourite ceremony came with the marriage of my youngest sister, sister number three in our family. I was only seven years old when I remember being in the over-decorated ceremonial wedding room. I still remember wearing my red jumper which my father bought me the same day of the wedding. My sister was the most beautiful bride, sitting with her girlfriends. No male members of my family were allowed in so they waited outside. My sister's friends teased and mocked me. I went to my sister with a comb and asked her if she would comb my hair. My sister's friends said, "What are you going to do tomorrow without your sister?"

I came to believe in God when I was only six years old. My mother was a very religious woman and she used to go the Temple every day to pray. It used to be only five minutes from our home. She came to know soon that I had a deep and insightful faith in God. One day, along with my mother and father present in one room, my mother told my father, "You know, your youngest son has got deep faith in God and he is only a six-year-old boy." My father looked at me and my mother and he said, "Very good, both of you. Go to the Himalayas and pray there." He said it sarcastically, and I looked at my father. Believe me, he got scared and left the room.

The most horrible moment of my life was when I was only an innocent seven-year old schoolboy. I was molested by an older boy, only eight years older than me. This boy was known to our family but not a relative, and used to live at a house far from my home. It was not intercourse, but by law, molestation. He returned the next day but by now I had come to know about his intentions. As I was growing, I tried to ignore him or avoid him, but when I achieved adolescence whenever I used to see him, I felt inside me as though I wanted to kill him. The reason of my hate and feelings was that he may be doing damage to someone else. The only thing that prevented me from doing this was my family, who were well respected. And the other reason was it was not worth going to jail for this worthless man.

I grew up and then came to the UK to become an Orthopaedic Consultant.

As all Asians, we have personally a great love of our home back in India. Every year, almost, we try to visit our home country. I used to do the same because I wanted to visit people back home. When I became a Consultant, my visits to India increased.

Once, I went to India on a routine annual visit. One of my relations came to see me. He said, "Do you remember the man who lives a few houses away from our home?", the man who abused me, "his only son has committed suicide." I became completely blank. My relation asked me what happened. I said nothing. After some time, our relation left. I cried in my room alone. Sometimes I went to the Temple and put my head on our Gods feet and said "thank you, so, you have done what is required." I came back. Believe me, until now, whenever the incident comes back haunting my memories, it's hard for me to control myself, asking my God, please help me, you have helped me always to overcome this abuse.

I believe all of these paedophile people, they have defective genes in their chromosomes. There is no way of preventing this from happening, nothing is effective. It is waste of time, manpower and money. Paedophile people are abnormal, they are all around.

Almost in all cases, they know their victim and hit when the time is bad for one innocent one. I feel I am sure one day some scientist will find these defective genes present in these people. If the gene present is found earlier then these culprits' acts can be prevented. I only pray to God. Please send someone with some wonderful discovery to save innocent people from these sick, ruthless, heartless people with abnormal behaviours, abnormal, unforgivable, unpardonable individuals to detect the defective gene before they act. Perhaps, even when they are born, early detection.

I found from an early age of my life that I am very good at studies. I always used to come out on top in studies.

My confidence grew with one incident I still remember. I was taking my Seventh Standard examination in my school. My uncle was staying at our home in Delhi because of his ill health due to a fracture of his right neck of femur. He was in Delhi for better treatment, because he came from a small city in UP India. He was recovering from the follow-up treatment at our home. He knew I was taking exams for the Seventh Standard. When I came back from school after my mathematics exam that day, he knew and he asked me how I got on. I said that I think I did well. He asked, "Show me your question paper." I showed him and I had already written answers to the questions on my question paper. I told my uncle to take this back to check the answers. The answers were given at the back of the book. He checked the answers to all the questions. I was telling him, with the book in his hand and without seeing the book myself. I was telling him the page where the question is, the number of the question. the book page and the answer already written by me on the question paper. He said that it was very good and said well done to me. My father, as usual, came back for his free weekend. My uncle perhaps was waiting for him. I was not at home. He called my father and told him everything about me. He said "for God's sake, take care of your son, he is a lot more than above par. He knew the whole book, pages of questions, their numbers and answers. It was beyond my belief. Please take care of him." My father, after a few days, he said, "Your uncle was saying about you, how good you are at studies." I said it was very nice of him.

After a few days, I asked my father, "I am doing quite well at school, why don't you send me to a Higher Standard School?"

He said, "My dear, I know, but I can't afford it. Already, two of your siblings, one brother, one sister, they are studying in Boarding School."

I told my father, "Don't worry father, I will try harder to do well at my school."

I came to know that I was not a normal human being at the age of twelve. I noticed that when one group of people were going in one way, I used to find myself going in the other direction.

Power possession in a human is well known. Power, if used by the person in a good way, according to God, that human being one day, sooner or later in life, is known as a legend. If the power gifted by God is not used in a good way, it leads to disastrous effects with harm to the individual.

Regarding palmistry, most are very correct, not fully, but it also depends on the palmist you see and how good he is. The same goes with astrology readings. Intuition and passion are also some of God's gifts, I was told by a palmist. For me, one of the things on my agenda on my holidays wherever I go is to see a palmist, along with other entertainments on holidays.

The intuitive power of God permits you to foresee things when you get up early in the morning, and easily know what sort of day you are going to have.

I landed in Riyadh, the capital airport in Saudi Arabia, for my job as a Consultant in Orthopaedics. This job was for one year as arranged by my English local agency. The moment I landed I knew I was going to stay for twelve years. Believe me, I left the job because of my children's education. I resigned after twelve years myself.

Regarding my family:

My father, my mother, two brothers, three sisters and myself who is the youngest in the family.

My father: Very good family man and a good husband. Held in great respect in our family and society. He was honest and hard working.
My mother: Lovely lady and liked by everyone. Very good mother.
My sisters: All very good sisters like the sisters one hopes for.
My brothers: All well-educated and lived their own lives, good as expected.

There is only one incident in my life when my father misbehaved with my mother verbally. I was present that whole night and my mother and I cried all night. My father left for his job. He came back home on his routine time off on the weekends. My father asked for me and my mother said, "He is hiding, he does not want to talk to you. Go and find him and talk to him." I was hiding behind the door. He eventually saw me looking around and said "Come out." I said "At first you say sorry to my mother and then talk to me." I even shouted at him, I said, "If you misbehave like this in future, I will never talk to you." He promised and kept his promise.

I started my primary school when I was five years old in 1955. My school was very basic. We used to sit on the floor and only had one blackboard at the front. There were no fans for fresh air but the windows of the classroom were always open. Being a good student, passing examinations was just a formality for me.

I never knew what holidays were. For us, hand to mouth living as a family, holidays meant rest at home and doing the school homework which I used to finish in the first two or three days.

The main problem during my childhood in our country of the Third World, was hygiene and heat. Heat was everywhere. In summer, temperatures sometimes shot up to forty-five degrees. Regarding hygiene, after the Independence, they had so many problems than to think about hygiene. That is why the mortality rate in infants and children was very high. It has come down but still requires much more to be done at present.

In my days, regarding the heat, the body gets acclimatised but what to do with a hygiene infection? As a child, you have to fight yourself or with medical assistance, if available. If the child survives and goes into his adult age, he has acquired antibodies against almost all diseases. He is perhaps a perfect example of a person who can survive in any harsh condition, anywhere in the world.

I was doing very well in school up to Eighth Standard. Then I was transferred from basic school to a high standard school in Delhi. I had to adjust with the other schoolboys who already had their education from the beginning in that school. I remember the story in our regular syllabus chapter book written by one of the most famous Indian writers. The name of the chapter was 'Home Coming'. It was about a boy who moved to a big city school from the village, a very bubbly young boy, but when he came back after spending some time with his relatives in the big city for a better education, he had a completely broken personality. In my case, somehow I survived this happening. If a child is transferred to a better school without adult supervision, something might have happened. But I was lucky to have only one blemish in the Tenth Standard of my school. I was told to repeat my English test after three months. I had to repeat this test along with another student. We both passed. He is also a retired doctor in Delhi. I was embarrassed to have to repeat my English test as my brother elder to me was, at the time, a Lecturer of English in Delhi University and we lived in the same house. Luckily I overcame this and passed my school Standards to join College.

Before giving details of my college life, I came to know when I was fourteen years of age that coming from a middle class family with no financial backing, the only way I could be a success in my life was to become friendly with my books. When I decided this, I felt that we were now three - myself, God and my books.

To enter Medical College, I had to do a one-year pre-medical education. I did this in Chandigarh, away from hospital, staying in a boys' hostel. During this tenure, I was conscious that my father was so hard-working and spending so much money. I put all my maximum efforts into applying for medical college.

I was obviously the most studious student in my hostel. This was the regime there: at the end of every year, the hostel administration used to give an award to the most hardworking student. I was first choice. Again, my intention helped me. I refused the award and the reason was that in case I didn't get an admission into medical college, what was the point in getting this award? The award was given to the second deserving candidate. My intention proved right again, I missed the entrance to medical college by only a few marks in the pre-med examination. This was not the end of the world. I came back to Delhi and joined one of the best colleges to get a Bachelor's Degree with the hope of entering medical school after receiving my Graduation Degree. I was focused to achieve this and I took my final examination after two years in Delhi College. Whilst waiting for the results to come, I went to my friend's house one evening and his sister-in-law answered the door. I asked, "Where is my friend?" She said, "Don't you know your result is out and you can go to the University to see your result, he has also gone there."

I came back home. My brother was at home. He sensed that something was wrong. He asked, "What is the matter?"

I said, "My result is out."

He said, "So, have you seen it?"

I said, "No."

He said, "Alright, we will go together to see your result!" I, along with my brother, went to Delhi University to see my result. As we were approaching the entrance of the University Hall where the result was put on the board, inside at the entrance of the long hall, all my friends came running to me and shouting, "Anish, you have come first in Delhi University and you have also got a First Class, you are the only one in the University." All my friends jumped on me and started kissing me.

I fell down. I said, "Please stop, my brother is standing nearby watching."

They said, "To hell, with your brother we are not going to leave you alone, the only one in Delhi University who has done this."

Two days after, my father came back home to Delhi. All members of the family were present in the courtyard of his house in total silence. My father felt that something had happened. He asked, "What is the matter?"

My sister approached him and said, "Do you know that your youngest son has broken the University record in the Bachelor of Science examination? He not only stood first but got a First Class and only your son could do this." My father was so surprised. He asked, "Are you serious?" Everybody said that it was true and I had done it. My father called me to come to him. He hugged me and patted me on my shoulder. This was the first time at the age of eighteen and I said to my God, so at last, he has realised that I am not an ordinary person. I passed my Bachelor of Science with a First Class and with a guarantee of admission to Medical College to become a doctor. Now, again, because nobody, or hardly anyone gets a First Class because it was unexpected I didn't fill out the entry form. To my surprise, my father filled out the form for me himself and signed for me. I automatically got the admission in Medical College.

I started my Medical College education, getting admission into Rhotak Medical College in Haryana, India. Everything was going normally, when, one day in the afternoon, I was asked by my class to go to the boardroom for a meeting with my Principal. I did not know what was happening. I was surprised to see my father waiting outside the boardroom. We went inside and my principal of the Medical College was sitting in the middle and explained to me that my father already knew. He said that the hospital administration was reluctant for me to continue my studies in this Medical College because I was from Delhi and not a domicile of Haryana. My father already brought so many documents with him to counter the Principal's accusation. My father, being a chief, always used to carry a gun and bullets around his waist. After an argument and counter arguments, the matter went on to the extent that he took out the gun. I stood still in one corner. He put the gun on the table in front of the Principal and said "I have given you all the written evidence, I don't know what to do next." He said, "I will come back after five minutes and tell you my verdict. There has to be one casualty." My Principal was very nervous and did not say anything for some time. Then, he looked at me and said, "Take this gun and the files and give them to your father and tell him it is alright for you to continue your Medical Studies." He said, "Make your father calm down."

I came out to my father who was waiting outside and he asked me, "What did your Principal say?" I told him that he said it was alright for me to continue my studies at this Medical College. I said that he told me to ask you to calm down.

I carried on being a hard-working good student and passed all my Medical Examinations without any problem.

Then, an unusual drama happened in my life. Before I give the details, I want to make something clear about our Professors or Heads of departments at the Medical Teaching Hospital at the time. They think they are not human beings and they don't even care about God. They think they are above God. When they become a Consultant, their body language, tone, movements, actions, attitude, outlook, understanding, emotions, behaviour, temper and living all changes. For them, they don't believe in God – only they are the Supremo. At their mercy are the poor junior student doctors. Junior doctors are the worst hit and the postgraduate students are the most mistreated.

After passing all the examinations, to achieve a doctor's degree, every medical student has to do one year's hospital training. After this they automatically get a final doctor's degree to practice anywhere. This one-year trainee period is a relaxing one because of the hard work one has done to pass all the examinations. There is no examination after this one-year training. But our Supremo Professor above God doesn't know whether to call them human beings. They could not tolerate the enjoyment of medical students during this one-year period when they are relaxed, thinking that after one year, they will automatically become a Consultant. The Supremoes got together in Haryana State Medical College which had nothing to do with the whole of India's Medical Colleges. They instituted themselves a mock exam to scare the trainee doctors.

This examination was to be conducted by those Supremo professors of our Rohtak Medical College. I never failed in Medical College examinations. I was one of the 125 students, boys and girls. These Supremos conducted the examination, all of them Heads of departments. I was the one who was victimised but I did not know why. The result was out. I never went to see the result. I thought it was just a formality but I was surprised to see my classmate, one of my friends, come to my hostel room and say in the boardroom, these Supremoes are waiting for you. I asked "What is he matter?" He said, "I don't know." I smelt a rat and decided to go the boardroom. I, alone, was the victim. I went in the boardroom to see all these

Supremos, sitting together in one room around the round table in silence. One of the Supremos opened his mouth and said, "We just want to let you know that you are required to repeat another three months as a trainee in the hospital before you get the Final Medical Degree to practice medicine."

I said, "I am sorry if I have done anything wrong." They told me no, but it was a board decision. I said that I knew they had decided and I requested that the Supremos please let me repeat these three months in a sister hospital of this main hospital. They, all of them, as if waiting, agreed unanimously.

I did this because of it being difficult to face my colleagues and medical paramedical staff because everybody knew me. I asked my friends why they picked on me. They said nothing else, they did not like your body language, they are Supremos above God. The only way this decision can be reversed is if you have any political connections. In front of politicians, these Supremos are like rats. Somehow, I passed in three months. It was the most agonising period of my life, seeing my father upset. I told my father, please control yourself, I can't see you like this. I told my father to be patient and let me get the degree first. So, after three months, automatically I got the degree. In simple words, victimisation by Supremos.

I came back to my father, eagerly waiting for me. He asked what happened and I said that I got it. I still remember the brightness in his eyes, which I never saw before. He asked me to show him the degree. I showed him the paper I got from hospital. He said, "Is this it?"

I said, "Father, you are not a medical man and this is how the system works. Don't worry, I have got Indian sweets for you, cheer up. Go to the Temple, I will go with you if you want." He said, "Go alone and thank God. Let me settle down and I will go very soon, later on."

Having worked in so many hospitals, I have come to know that the best medical doctors are all from India Institute Delhi, they are at par or above par compared to anywhere in the world. When I passed my MBBS, at that time the whole batch from this college passed Medical Final Examination including all the candidates went to the USA, nobody came back and settled in Delhi. The worst doctors from Medical College are the ones with connections to politicians. The next below-par medical doctors are the ones who get admission with donations. The worst as reported recently are the doctors practising with false degrees they get easily from Asian countries. This is very much in the news these days as I am writing this book.

Before I became a registered doctor to practice, my father, with the help of his friend who had contact with Governor of Delhi, arranged a job for me to work in one of the three star-type hospitals in Delhi. This was a favour done by a friend of my father who's granddaughter was to become a family member in the future. Unfortunately due to these wicked Super-God Professors who extended my training, this job was given to somebody else. But I think this was a blessing in disguise for me. The hospital was a three star-type and in very bad surroundings. It was near a big vegetable market. My father asked me, "What do you want to do now?" I said, "Don't worry father, you relax. I am a registered doctor, I will find my own way."

I knew, in India, to get a job, there are two ways. One very easy way to get job is through any political connection. The other way is to approach the clerk of the hospital. The one whom the director depends on for all his important work. My option was evident. So, I started looking for a job as a Junior Doctor in Delhi. I used to go to multiple hospitals everyday. Eventually, I impressed one of the VIP Hospital Clerks. He took me to his Chief Hospital Director. The Director took only a few minutes to decide for me to start work in his hospital from the next day.

I came back and my father was shocked to know that I managed to get the job in a VIP Government hospital. I said, "Father, leave it to me. It is only the beginning. You only pray." I understood myself that I am not only honest, hard-working and intelligent, but also I am quite clever when dealing with difficult situations.

Before I start discussing my future career as a doctor, I want to mention that up until now, my memories go back to the day when I Graduated from Delhi University.

I saw my name on the Merit List Name Board in the main prize distribution wall and only my name was displayed that year, 1969: Anish Kumar Kurar, 1st Class 1st Delhi University. When the ceremony was held, I was specially invited to receive my prize trophy from the Dean of the University. Those memories are always with me. At the age of eighteen, to read my name on the University Merit Board. When I received the award, my name was called and I walked from my chair to the podium. I was just walking straight as if everything had stopped. When I received the trophy, I started coming back and then I heard loud clapping from the massive audience in the hall. At the time, I felt as if my eardrums would burst. Somehow, I managed to come back to my chair. After the ceremony, coming out of the hall, I met my Zoology Head of Department. We both stood apart, looking at each other. We did not know what to say or how to express ourselves, but both our eyes said everything and without saying a word, we passed.

After this, my real life started, the first day as a doctor at the age of twenty-five. I started my job in the Department of Surgery, VIP Hospital, Delhi. My registrar told me to finish my work on the ward and come to the theatre to help. I did as advised and went to the theatre after work. My chief surgeon was operating with my registrar as an assistant. They were doing surgery on a patient's spine. My registrar asked me to scrub up and come and help in the operation. The surgeon completed the main operation and asked my registrar to close the wound as normal practice. Before leaving the theatre, he asked my registrar to take a photograph before he started closing the operative field. The surgeon left my registrar and did the rest after we came out. I asked my registrar why the chief said to take a photograph before we close the wound. My registrar said because the patient is going to die. I, without hesitation, asked why, if the patient was going to die, did he operate? My registrar said, the chief said if we don't operate, who will? I told myself, good God, Lord, you gave me the perfect day to start my medical career.

I continued with my job doing well, but again, as usual, something had to happen. We, as normal, went for our evening round on the ward. Myself, with my registrar and my chief at his home. We saw one patient who was day three post-operative. The patient still had a drain in. My registrar told me to take out the drain, just pull it out after sterilizing the operative site. I did as advised. The moment I pulled the drain out, immediately, dark red blood gushed out from the wound. I called my registrar who was nearby. By the time he came, the whole bed was soaked with blood and there was so much blood on the floor. My registrar said that this was a secondary haemorrhage and to just put a pack on the wound and press. He went to inform my consultant. The consultant came within six hours and he asked to arrange for the patient to go to theatre for exploratory surgery. We found only oozing from the operative site after normal packing was done with closure of the wound and with intention to take the patient to theatre after their condition improved.

Unfortunately, the patient died in two days. A big complaint was lodged by the family of the deceased. A complaint with the specific name of my chief and his most junior doctor who had not completed six months of his services. My senior consultant got so furious to see his name with mine, as the responsible doctors for the patient's death. I knew beforehand that this is a case of post-operative infection. But as usual, the senior has to put blame on someone and in this case it was me, the obvious choice. My boss's behaviour totally changed after the complaint of the chief came to the notice of everyone in the department. It was my first job. Somehow, I survived and finished six months in surgery.

My next job was at the same hospital in General Medicine with the number one consultant taking care of important Indian VIPs for their medical care.

The first day of my job in medicine was on call with a registrar related to a politician and my consultant at the VIP Hospital, Delhi. Normal emergency admission is 24 hours. My registrar and I took round before our consultant came. After our round, my registrar said, "Well, I am going, you take care, you are in charge now." He said, "Don't worry when the consultant comes, he will come to the ward, stand in the centre and will ask you about the patients admitted. He will not go to the patient's bed. You tell him about the patient, what you have written in your notes about the patient in your book."

I said, "Look, it is my first day."

He said, "Don't worry."

He left and I knew this registrar was related to the politician living in the VIP government bungalow. I could not say or do anything. As

I did not sleep the whole night, I left after the round. I went to my room, waited for the consultant to come. On my round, I noticed that one of the patient's had some trouble breathing. I reviewed the medicine as suggested by the registrar.

I went to my room to wait for my consultant. I don't remember when I went to sleep because I did not sleep the whole night. I was on call with my registrar. The sister knocked on the door and woke me up and said that my consultant had arrived for the round. I woke up. As told by the registrar, I stood in the centre of the ward and I gave him the verbal ward round as told by the registrar. He said, "Well done," and left for his home. I noticed that the lady with breathing difficulty was not moving as much as before. I had this in mind. From the end of my round, I went to my centre table to write notes of the patients in their file. I remember before I wrote the notes, that I went to see this lady with breathing difficulty. The moment I was going to the patient, two of the patient's relatives came to me and said, we think our relation is no more. I said, are you talking of the bed number so and so. They said yes, but how do you know? I kept quiet deliberately with no change of my expression. I told myself, she was dead when the consultant was taking rounds.

I shouted for the nurse to bring the cardiac massage tray. She understood and rushed to the bed of the patient. We did the routine resuscitation. I knew it was a formality but she was dead on the ward round. My registrar was not present and the consultant was taking ward rounds from centre of ward without going to patient's beds. This was my first day as a junior doctor in medicine. My faith in God became stronger.

This registrar of mine was a relative of a politician, but he was not bad in his medical knowledge. He had postgraduate degree from one of the good hospitals. But as I mentioned, this registrar had a problem, he was a drug addict, hooked on injectable drugs. I came to know about this soon because this drug addiction can't be hidden from regular nearby people, especially doctors, like myself.

I came to know very soon and he also became aware of this. He knew I knew, so he became quite open with me and within a few days, he became very friendly with me. One day, he brought a few injections to my room. I was not working and he knew I was sitting at home. He also knew I didn't like drugs but I agreed and he injected me with an intramuscular double dose of morphine. He told me after the injection. In my room, at the same time, he also injected himself with a double dose. He said, this is a normal dose for us so don't worry. After the injection he immediately left. I did not like it but did it because of my new job, the consultant being the caretaker of the most important VIP hospital in India. What is there to say, I just went to bed, had a very nice sleep because of double dose of morphine. The next day, we met together in a routine way. He said, "What did you do afterwards?"

I said I had a nice sleep. I asked, "What about you?"

He said, "I had a really good time in the evening."

I said. "Did you go anywhere?"

He said. "No, I was at home enjoying my garden with my dog." He said, "I did something different yesterday."

I asked, "What did you do?"

He said, "I injected my dog with a double dose of morphine."

I said, "Oh my God, is he still alive?"

He said, "Yes, yes."

I said, "Why did you do that?" I said to myself, I should not ask him this question. He said that after injecting the dog with the morphine, he walked normal for some time, then his walk got wobbly as if the drug was acting like alcohol. Suddenly, the dog fell like a block on the ground. He left him in the garden and saw him before he went to sleep after some time.

I said, "For God's sake, leave the poor dog alone." I continued with my job. This one-year trainee job is very tough, demanding hard work and at the same time you have to learn. I found learning in India is self learning. Who is interested in teaching you? Nobody has got any time and why should they, even if they are supposed to do this, but who cares?

I believe this has been happening since my birth. To become a good doctor, you have to be very sincere, hard-working, believe in yourself and be intelligent. In India, you don't hope for any help from anybody. Everything depends on yourself. No doubt the story

Alcoholic Doctor

changes when you have achieved in the future, if God has helped you. Then it is quite interesting to see how people around you change. I was fortunate because of my hard work, I have seen all this. I continued my job in the VIP Hospital as normal. One day, I was on call for ward duties. As normal, my politician connection registrar, at five o'clock, left for his home, telling me if there was any problem, contact him at home. I was doing paperwork at my desk after my registrar left. I noticed two people standing close to the sister's desk, one holding the telephone. On the ward, I knew that there was only one lady in a bad condition in her fifties. The sister wanted to use the phone but these two people wouldn't let her use the phone. They said, "No, we are waiting for a phone call from the Prime Minister's son, Sanjay Gandhi."

The sister got scared and left to use the other phone. In the meantime, the phone rang. The two people talked to the person said to be Sanjay Gandhi for some time. Then they asked me to speak to him because he wants to talk to me regarding their patient on our ward. I had no choice because there was nobody around me more senior to help. I said I'd come and took the phone call. He asked me why I was speaking in English. He asked where did I learn English? He was speaking in Hindi, our mother language. I immediately understood. I kept quiet. He talked about the only serious patient on the ward and told me to make sure that the patient was alright and put the phone down. By now, I knew how these politicians behaved. I continued my job, as I was supposed to do on the ward alone. I never informed anyone the whole night I was up and it has become routine for me when on call to get rest for a few hours. That is called an easy night. At least, I had slept for a few hours.

In the morning, everybody came. Luckily, the patient's condition improved to the extent that she had breakfast. All the staff people working on the ward were thinking that they may not see the lady in the morning alive. I thought again that God came to my rescue. Our VIP Consultant normally came out everyday for afternoon tea, and met all the staff members in person so they could give him the details of what happened the day before. It was a routine report, then my registrar told the Consultant, "Sir, Anish got a phone call from Sanjay

Gandhi regarding the sick lady we discussed in the meeting." He said, "What are you saying. What happened?"

I said I had nobody to help me, I had to take the phone call.

He said, "Why did not you ring me at home?"

The assistant consultant said, "Nobody was expecting to see this lady alive in the morning but we were shocked to see her sitting on the bed having breakfast." She said, "We don't know what Anish did."

I said, "I don't know but I did not sleep." Everybody in the meeting said, go and have some sleep and take the afternoon off.

From that day, my consultant's attitude towards me completely changed in a positive way. I mentioned my registrar was addicted to drugs. Forty years ago, it was very easy to get injections from ICU when I was working in India in VIP hospital. These junior doctors used to steal from ICU. They used to use them for themselves, only a few of us knew. Some of the doctors used to use this to have fun with the girls. One of my close friends who was quite good looking and handsome was very addicted to drugs and he used to use them for entertainment to have fun with a girl. This friend of mine was later caught doing wrong with a female patient on the ward. He had to answer about the incident to an inquiry team in front of the board. As in many instances, the case closed with warning to him to cover it up. The same doctor was good enough to go to the United States to work as a doctor did the same thing. This time it was publicised by the media because a complaint was lodged by minor relatives.

He was given the option to face punishment and stay in the USA or to go back to India. He preferred to return to India. One of my friends known to him, he said he is now a retired consultant radiologist living in India. In my days, forty years ago, doctor's earned respect in society. For young doctors, girls used to fancy them, especially if they were handsome.

In our doctor's residence it seemed like there was a competition going on. From whose room do the maximum number of girls come out? My room was one of those I realised, from our lift supervisor, who used to accompany people using the lift for security reasons. One day, I came back from my duty going to my room in our lift. The man said, "If you don't get angry, can I ask a favour from you?"

I thought maybe he is asking for some money. I said, "Go on."

He said, "Sir, so many girls come in and out of your room, can you oblige me also?" I said to myself, oh my God, I never thought this. It cannot happen. I kept quiet.

My year long job finished with good and bad memories of learning in my trainee period. To get admission into Medical College was very tough, everyone's first choice was to become a doctor. The vacancies to get admission into Medical College are few in this massive, over-populated country. So, from the start, one coming to Medical College has above par intelligence. That is why the graduates from the Medical Colleges are very good, especially if they come out of the country and get higher education in other advanced countries in the medical profession. However, the worst treatment given to a doctor can be the one doing a postgraduate Fellowship to get a higher qualification in India by a supremo consultant.

I remember when I was still there in boy's hostel before my graduation, one of the postgraduate students, jumped from the third floor three days before his examination,. This, I am sure, was because of the worst Surgeon Supremo Consultant in our hospital, known to everyone as a bad man. There are also other examples who can't face these Super Gods. But I can't say all the Supremo Consultants are bad, but there are very few good. I believe this profession is too demanding. If you can't cope, then the answer is simple, change your profession. I keep telling my son this. He is also a Fellow of the Royal College of the United Kingdom. He is getting trained in one of the London hospitals.

After one year in the VIP Hospital, I worked for a few months as a junior doctor in a private well-known hospital in Delhi, before I got a permanent job in one of the dispensaries, a Delhi Government job. I was a young doctor, single, doing a job earning money which I started seeing for the first time. My own money, my earnings. During this time, I learnt the art of becoming a friend with alcohol. As I mentioned, this is in the genes of the chromosome cell of the person whois born with this. I had a strong liking for alcohol but I did not like any other narcotics, especially drugs. I think I was only twenty-four years old at this point. We were four then, myself, God, books and my last friend, alcohol. Dispensary standards in India are very low. This job before coming to the UK was so easy and on top of it I was making good money as if I was getting money without doing anything.

I was really enjoying my life. Every day a party like a prolonged endless Christmas. Everybody was noticing but nobody would say anything to me. Anyway, I would not listen to anybody. There was one lady doctor working in the same dispensary, she said, "Anish, the way you live, these people, they won't let you live here. Go away from here. Go to London." She especially mentioned London, I don't know why. My friend got papers to fill in to apply for a job in the UK. He also wanted to go to the UK himself, perhaps that was the reason. Anyway, he helped me and I got the job. My lady doctor who told me to go away and go to London was so happy and excited and said "I am being serious now, my marriage is after three days. If you agree, I will cancel my marriage. I can't wait." I said to myself, look, this is a nice happy doctor in Delhi, I don't know what is going to happen to me in the UK, only God knows. My principle is that if you can't make her comfortable, then at least I should not make her uncomfortable. I kept quiet. She probably understood what was my answer and why.

My friend told me, "Anish, as you are going to the UK, why don't you use the rest of your time here in India? Enjoy yourself. You don't know how much hard work you have to do to settle there." I fully agreed and the next day, I went to the WMO Office for an interview to work as a Malaria Control Programme Worker in different parts of India. I had training before starting the job. I was lucky as my selection was to control Malaria in Mizoram City, Lunglae. This area, near the Bangladesh border, is a very volatile area because Mizo local people are fighting in India for their own state to become autonomous. I signed my contract for my job with WHO which also included the care of my driver and vehicle at my disposal, all the time paid by WHO.

I could not ask for better than this. My flight was from Delhi to Calcutta to Gaali to Guwahati for a brief stay there, then to Shillong – the tourist place of India, near the Darjeeling Tea Gardens state. Here was our sister office of the WHO's main office in Delhi. From Shillong,

I was given the responsibility to look after a local Mizoman driver and a jeep with WHO nameplates. I felt as if I had got a senior job in the Indian Military Force at the age of twenty-seven. I was off to Aizawl Mizoram and then a three hours' journey to Lunglei, my place of work. Mizoram is full of lush green meadows, low hills which are alltotally unexplored because of the local rebellion fighting against the Indian Government. While going to Lunglei, I asked the driver, "What are these birds flying above?" He said that they were cocks flying, chasing hens and males fighting each other. I had never seen the cocks flying in air so fiercely. Mizoram is such a beautiful part of India. When I was going to my final destination it looked varied because it was the first time I had seen this. I felt as if I was on some other planet.

There was very good security because of the high military presence to counter rebels. Hills on the one side and the other side, and in between them, a deep ditch. When we looked down from the road, we couldn't see the bottom. I have never seen such tall bamboo trees. If the jeep fell in the ditch, nobody would find the bodies. We would only be a good meal for the local wild animals.

I reached Lunglei and my place of stay. My driver was also staying on the same ground near my own house. There was some place separate for him and a place for the jeep to be kept for security. In the evening, after travel, I saw it was all hazy in my room, I thought maybe the house was on fire. I ran out to my driver's house. I said that I thought the house was on fire and he said, "Come, we see." He came to my house with me and he started laughing. He said, "This is not fire, these are clouds in your room."

I said, "What?"

He said, "Sir, you are really from Delhi. You have not seen this? You will see heavy rain soon. This is a signal." Then he left. I had some more to drink and felt clouds in my hand and put my hands above clouds. I had seen clouds only from the plane window. I felt that I was so lucky to come to this area but the military guards were not allowed to travel alone after six in the evening. If one has to travel in an emergency, this has to be planned and the convoy moves under supervision. One of the Brigadier-Generals was ambushed and killed. I saw the place where he was killed because the military had made some sort of remembrance for him. Mizo people are like Mongolians in appearance, brown to fair, medium height, very nice, very friendly, fun and loving from the small houses around. Every evening they would be playing loud music and there would be a party in almost every house every day.

I could hear very melodic music played on Western and Asian instruments. In the evening and early night, it looked like the whole town was in a festive mood. The best thing I remember is their homemade liquor made from rice. I have not tasted it since I have left Mizoram years ago. At least I tasted it for which I am grateful to God.

I was invited by the local Mizoram City Head, they arranged a small party for me. There were other important local people and I was the chief guest. They were so humble, generous, respectful and served me a special feast. In the feast, whenever they invite any guest like this, they serve dog meat. I believe in Gods on this earth and all religion. I don't mind eating anything, including all Chinese dishes. I enjoyed everything, including the dog meat. Then I thought, this is reason that no dog is seen on the roads or anywhere else, apart from pets. The animals they hate are monkeys because they think they resemble monkeys when they grow old.

I was also lucky to be invited to the military regiment. I knew before that military people, wherever they are, are given a place to stay. They change the place they occupy and make their own paradise. I happened to go near their tents. I saw almost in all the tents that there were some bottles of whisky half finished, closed or open on the table. I still remember their nice cooked Indian bread and chickpeas, potato curry, along with other items for breakfast for which we were invited.

I remember, apart from my work on the control of malaria in that area, one day my driver asked me, "Sir, do you want to see the Bangladesh border?"

I said, "Why not? I have come all the way from Delhi to this place, let me take some more memories of this place back."

He said, "We go in the evening before sunset. Sir, I know you like your drink, have some before we go to the border." I did not understand and I asked myself why is he saying this?

I said, I have drink every evening before my supper anyway. This young Mizo driver being local knew all the places. He took me not far away from my place of stay to the Bangladesh border. He said, "Sir, I go to the local shop. You go and enjoy, see the river in front and sandy beach. Go around and have fun, I see you in one hour. Then we go back."

This river was very nice, flowing from Bangladesh to India and the place called Dimagiri. This is the place where the British also entered India and is one of the places that has the best fish, they say in the world, which comes from Bangladesh and travels to India. The best fish I mention, but what I saw on the riverside in the evening still haunts my memories, even at the age approaching seventy. All the middle-age, young women were taking a bath in river and took off all their clothes. I stood still, but far away, watching. I could not believe it. I said to myself, I have seen the Mizo paradise place, including clouds but what on earth is this? Now I realised why my Mizo driver said, have some drinks before we go to the river. Luckily, my driver came back. He asked, "Do you want to go anywhere else?" I asked myself, is there anything else to see now?

I asked my driver, "Can you be kind enough to take me to my house?" He smiled. The moment I reached my place, I could see only the bottom of the bottle. I stood up, went flat on my bed only to wake up again in the morning and continue the day again, but what I saw still I see so many times, especially when I am in good mood after drinking.

Now it was time for me to go to London as I finished my WHO job. I am approaching seventy years of my age. I have seen a number of countries, including Pakistan. For me, the three months I spent in Mizoram stand out as too good, too large from my memories. After seeing so many countries, the best one for me is Kashmir. Not the commercial Kashmir, but the interior of Kashmir, which is unexplored. It takes me back to my belief in the perseverance of nature by super power. Because of the infighting in Kashmir and the bad relations with Pakistan, tourists are scared to go there. In a way, this is very good for nature. Greenpeace don't have to think about this. Some nature preservation is due to the border areas of India. They are second to Kashmir and are equivalent to any European tourist place but they're very natural. All these areas of Mizoram, Nagaland, Tiripura where tourists are too scared to go because of rebel activities are real natural places. I hope these places remain like this. I am sure nature as usual takes care of itself.

Now is the time to go back to the UK, London, again. My problem was the money. I had earned and spent it all on my enjoyment. Everybody came to know, including a few of the parents with eligible daughters. They approached my father and said for him to ask me about marriage and if he agrees they can arrange for everything for me to go the UK. My father told me this. I asked my father, "Father, you are so good, would you do this?"

He said, "Never. I will let them know." Only seven days left until my start date and I had no plane ticket. I was drinking at five o'clock in the afternoon when my sister's son came to see me. He said, "Doctor Shahib, you have started drinking so soon, why? Is everything alright?"

I said, "Have a chair and make a drink for yourself, however much you want."

He said "Tell me, what is it?" I said, "You know I am leaving in seven days' time and I don't have a ticket to go. Just imagine…I am youngest in my family. All the others are working and nobody asked me about my ticket, only my father who has not got the money. He is so worried."

"Is there anything else bothering you?" he said

I said, "No, that is the only thing."

He said, "Alright, let me have a drink."

I said, "Please help yourself or do you want me to make it for you?"

He said, "I will have my drink. Listen to me, you be ready by ten o'clock in the morning, I will come on my bike and get you the ticket tomorrow. Now relax, drink as much as you want, but be ready by ten in the morning." He came on time. He took me to one of the banks in Delhi.

He explained to the manager whom he knew beforehand the purpose of our visit.. The bank manager asked for an accountant to come and advised him to issue ten thousand rupees. I said, "Seven thousand is enough," equivalent to one hundred pounds at that time, forty years ago.

Alcoholic Doctor

He said, "Keep a little more if required. Come back to me, don't worry whenever you have money after you settle in London, give it back to the bank but make sure you are comfortable and settled in the UK first." I thanked him for his kindness and what he had done for me. Now, it was time for me to go the UK.

Then it was the time when I said goodbye to all forever. Before departure, as normal, there is always a small party when all the relatives and friends, come home to say goodbye and have meal and a drink. Only a few accompany the one leaving to the final departure at the airport. At the airport, I was like just like anybody, just on a mission to go to London and start a new life. I did not know what was going to come ahead of me. My youngest sister came to me at the airport and said, "Please go and see your father, he is crying in one corner." I went to him.

I said to my father, "If you don't want me to go, I will not go."

He said, "Are you mad? I am so happy. I never thought one of my sons who is a doctor is going to work in a London hospital. Please go, I will pray for you here in India."

Then it was the beginning of a totally new life – an adult re-born. The flight from Delhi Indira Gandhi Airport to London stopped for three days in Kabul because of a transit flight which was the cheapest available forty years ago. It was my first international flight. It proved to be blessing in disguise for me. I could see Afghanistan and came to know about the people. The flight from Delhi to Kabul took about two hours. From Kabul, we were taken to the hotel, a three-star, in the middle of Kabul surrounded by houses, it was obviously a posh area. At that time, Afghanistan was occupied by Russians and the airport was surrounded by tanks, troops andsoldiers everywhere. Local Afghan people hated them. I came to know this after talking with local English speaking Afghans.

Afghan people are the most beautiful people. Next, I noticed the Lebanese. All rich Arabians in the old times migrated to Lebanon. Before the civil war in Lebanon it used to be the best country in Arabia, but not now, it has totally changed. Afghan people are so beautiful and handsome, that you can't take your eyes off them. I was lucky to arrive in the hotel on the same day as a marriage party of local

Afghanis taking place in the evening. The head of the marriage party invited all of us. They knew that the crew, staff and people going to London are marrying at the same hotel. It was very nice to attend the marriage party. Before starting my life in England, why not enjoy a marriage party in Afghanistan? They offered us food, drinks and there was also music and dance, a great evening for all of us.

Afghan people are very nice, tall, handsome and beautiful, especially the people living locally in hilly areas who were very polite. We were allowed to go and see the town from the hotel but at our own risk. I, being young and alone, did not care and took a cab and went around. Afghan food is not to my liking: thick bread, vegetables and dry meat cooked. Although Afghan dry fruits are very famous and well known all over. One main source of income of Afghans at the time came from the cannabis grown in big areas which was distributed all over the world for money. The finest quality of cannabis can be grown in Afghanistan and is grown for their survival. That is why Afghanistan people are still there in spite of occupations by some kings, warriors, countries, but they all failed.

Afghanistan is mostly a dry place. Deserts and hills with oases where the main narcotic crops were grown under the control of local Afghans, in spite of United States occupation, after Russia had already left with a known failure.

I started my job with a one-month attachment under the supervision of a consultant in Birmingham at the Good Hope Hospital, UK. After two weeks my consultant came to me and told me that he was not happy with me. I asked the reason and he said "you can appeal against my decision." He did not give me any answers to my question. I had arrived in this country from India with a work permit visa. I applied to the GMC, England. I was asked to come for an interview in the boardroom which was in Leicester Square, London. I arrived on time and went up to the board room. The boss opened the door as if he knew that I was the one to go in. In the big room with a table and chairs, it was only me and him. He offered me the chair and asked me what happened. I said the supervisor consultant was racist. His face went red and he burst out and said "Don't say that." There was pin drop silence for one minute. He looked at my face which was expressionless because I have been used to a lot of these meetings. After a minute he said, we'll give you another chance for you to do an attachment in Derby this time. I got up, thanked him and left the boardroom.

I started my new attachment of one month under a very senior respectable surgeon consultant in Derby. After one month, he gave me a letter so that I could start my regular job as NHS Doctor. I got a job the next day for one month in the same hospital.

After this, I got a regular job in Neurosurgery at Morriston Swansea Hospital. I did six months normal without any incidents to note. My job automatically extended for another six months. After one year, I saw my bank balance sheet. I never had so much money to my name in my bank as I come from a middle class Indian family. I went to administration and I resigned. My administration asked me what is the matter, what happened, why do you want to leave? I said, "I am homesick. I want to go home for some time."

The administration said, "It is your decision. We were thinking of promoting you because of your work."

I said, "Please let me go."

They said, "It is so, you can go. In case you come back, please be in touch with us."

I thanked them and bought my first flight back to Delhi. All my relatives and my friends were surprised to see me back so soon. Normally, when someone goes to foreign country they never return back so soon. I said to myself, let them guess. I have to live my own life, nobody helped me before now. Now that I don't need any help, why should I bother. I am the type of person who will never care about anybody until I think it is right. Then I will do it. As I have never seen money, I wanted to enjoy my money. It is only in young age when you can enjoy your money. You don't have to wait for your retirement to enjoy your savings if you have any. Some of my friends asked me, have you given up on medicine, started some business in the UK? I just ignored all.

The word of my arrival back spread like wildfire. All my relatives and friends came to see me again. I distributed all the gifts which I had brought from England for them. The most important person who came to see me was my lady street sweeper early in the morning. I was having breakfast and she came and showed so much gratitude and love that it is was if her own son has come back after a prolonged time. She said somebody told me you have come back. "I asked really, my son has come back from London. Now he is big London man, I must go and see him." She came and I was really delighted as she knew me from my days of childhood. I wanted to hug her but I could not. Instead, I stood up and tears came out of her eyes. I said, "Please stop." I gave her one hundred rupee note to her and told her, have a party with her children. She looked at the note, kept looking at that as if I had given her a hundred pounds.

In our street, we had fourteen houses. She went to each house, showing them the hundred rupee note, telling everyone, my son, Nisha, from London, has come on holidays and look what he has given me. My street mates told me, even the sweepers are now singing songs for you. It has only been one year of your stay in the UK. We don't know what is going to come next. I said to myself, forget about everything until I have no money left, enjoy yourself.

We, in the evening, anybody who wants to have drinks and other bits of food, just come to see me. Every day will be a party.

It was a well-known fact that Doctor Shahib liked whisky which was always present at my place. When anybody, neighbours, or my friends were short of whisky or the shop was closed, they used to come and borrow whisky, whatever was left that day.

I had already thought about this, that when I came back on holiday, I would go to Kashmir. I told my family and my friends that I was going to Kashmir because I had not seen it. My elder brother and one of my friends said, "We will also go with you. We will give you company there." I said that was very nice of them. It would be great fun.

It was my first visit to Kashmir. We stayed in a five-star hotel in the centre of the city near Dal Lake. The capital of Kashmir is a commercial one. Apart from the Dal Lake, I did not like anything in the Srinagar Capital. The Kashmir food cooked nicely is very good, quite different. A few of the special dishes you can only get in Kashmir. They know how to cook, it is their old authentic way of cooking. Some of these dishes take quite a few hours to cook.

I have read in a book, regarding the natural beauty of Kashmir. Eventually, I found it when we went right into the interior of Kashmir by car, a few hours journey far away from the capital of Kashmir. When I saw the interior of Kashmir, I realised why Keating once said, "If there is any paradise on earth, it is only Kashmir, Kashmir, Kashmir."

I have travelled so much now and I still have not seen any other place like the interior of Kashmir. Other famous European tourist places, they are very good but this was no comparison. Natural, unexplored, preserved by natural means of their own infighting and fights going on between India and Pakistan. People are now, these days, asking for trouble when they go to these places.

This is how nature works. When it wants to preserve itself, nature knows how. In this case, infighting and fights at the border for more than seventy years are still unsolved. The way it looks like now is like it would never be resolved which is bad for human beings killing each other but very good for nature.

Living in the five-star hotel was quite good and I stayed for two further days on a boat with all the facilities, even for cooking. The boat was like a house floating on water. There were boats surrounded by water with so many different flowers, fauna and locals belonging to Kashmir. There were local -grown, natural types of lilies in the water with birds of all sizes and colour, chattering around. I found my stay in the boat more enjoyable than hotel.

Kashmir people are very good looking but not as compared to the Afghans and Lebanese. They are definitely better looking and handsome. God made Kashmir people very nice, soft spoken and friendly, because most of the money comes from abroad, tourism is the number one source of revenue. Other means are there but they are different. I remember one incident, staying in the five-star hotel in Srinagar, with my brother and my friend. We had drinks in the room. My brother and my friend told me to go to dinner room downstairs and order something which I like. I came down, the waiter came to ask me for order. I asked him about the favourite dishes. He said about few. He said, "These are very good local Kashmir dishes."

I said, "Bring all of them."

He said, "Are you sure?"

I said, "Yes, my friend and my brother are joining me."

He said, "That is alright then." He brought dishes and laid them on the long table. In the meantime, my friend and my brother came down from the room and asked me if I'd ordered dishes with the waiter.

He said, "Yes, he ordered these." My friend and brother looked at the laid table full of dishes on the top.

They said, "My God, who is going to eat all of this?"

I said, "I told him to bring good dishes. He brought them all." They laughed and explained to the waiter, "Look, he had a few drinks. You do one thing, leave the best one, take the rest of them."

He said, "No problem, I have done this before also. Sir is new to this country."

I still remember this meal sometimes in my dreams. I wake up to see, Thank God, nothing on the table, it is in my dream.

We came back from Kashmir. Again, we had a party every day. Finally, I noticed my bank balance was telling me to go back to England. I stayed for three months and enjoyed to the full extent. Every good thing has to come to an end for me and I automatically get called to work, to earn money again Now I knew what you can do with money if you planned properly.

I packed my luggage and came back to the UK. Getting a job now was no problem this time. Without much delay, I got a job as an Orthopaedic Consultant near Newcastle for one year. This time, I had decided to take the Part One FRCS exam and get it out of the way. When I I told my colleagues they all laughed. They said, "You have just come back, calm down, the Fellowship exams are not that easy. You will waste time and money." As usual, I ignored them and I started working for the Part One FRCS examination in my hospital and my books. After one year, I applied for the Part One examination in Dublin.

Asians have very good memories. If someone's memory is good, then the exam result is obvious. In this case, one does not require any coaching. I went to Dublin for my written exam which had negative marking. I answered more than the required questions. I knew I couldn't fail and I passed the written. The next day was the oral examindation for the candidates. There were two professors in Dublin examining me, asking questions. I was replying like a parrot. They would stop in between the questions for some time. Eventually, one of the examiners asked me, "Are you from the all India Institute, Delhi Medical College?" I knew what he was looking for.

I lied, I said, "I am."

He said, "I knew you were from there because I've been to that college. I know the students from that college." I did not feel bad that I lied because I didn't think did any harm to anyone. This was the first time I lied. But I had learnt that where I told truth so many times, I suffered because of my truthfulness.

My flight back to England was the next day. After the examination, I had to spend the evening and night in Dublin. I bought some whisky and decided to enjoy a Chinese meal to celebrate before the result was released which I had planned to see early in morning when the university gate opened, to see my name on the pass list on the board. The night before, I did not sleep at all. At seven o'clock in the morning, I put on my slippers and went to the university, my hotel was near the main University of Dublin. At 7AM sharp , the gate opened. Myself with few more candidates, mainly local ones, went in to see the names on the board. My name was right there. I looked up and said, thank God, I knew you wouldn't let me down. My intuitions also proved correct again. The message I got was to believe in this more in future as you have been doing before.

I came back to my hospital and everybody already knew the results. I didn't know how. The administration called afterwards when I was working, they said, "Congratulations for passing the examination in Dublin, but there is bad news for you from Delhi." They informed me that my father was no more, and they had received the message when I was taking the examination and they did not want to disturb me. They said, relax, have a sip of water. They told me, if I wished, if I wanted to attend my father's last rights ceremony that I was entitled to go as the hospital allows for so many days off. The decision is mine. I said, please let me go. They said, whenever I am ready, I can go to Delhi.

I immediately booked my flight to Delhi. I came home and met all my family members. In Hindu tradition, the death ceremony lasts fourteen days. I attended with all the known persons who came to attend the ceremony. I remember only one incident during this period when the ceremony was going on, one of the known ladies to our family, came to me and said, "I just wanted you to know, that your uncle, her husband, also passed away a few days ago."

I said, "I am sorry to hear this."

Another thing she said, "I wanted to tell you now that your father is no more. He used to love you so much, you being youngest in the family. He was so proud of you. He used to tell everybody that you know my son is a doctor in London. He remembers all of us here back home so much, we are always in touch with him."

After my father's final rites were over in India, I came back to my working place in England. I finished my job near Newcastle, in Consett Hospital. I was looking to get a job straight away in one of the hospitals in Central London as a Junior Doctor in the Orthopaedic Department. To start with, this job was for six months but I got an extension, because of my work. After six months, I was promoted to a registrar post in Orthopaedics. At that time, I was taking the final Fellowship Royal College of Surgeons' examination. Everybody knows this is the toughest exam in the world. The Royal College believe it maintains the highest standard. I believe this is correct. They also know that if the candidate gets the Fellowship Final FRCS degree, he may go back to his country. If he is not up to their standard, it may spoil their name. Part One of the Fellowship examination was easy for me but I knew I did not have any postgraduate qualifications from India. It would be tough for me. The pass percentage was very low, only eight percent. The candidates believe that the first to pass are from the UK, then the Europeans, followed by Arabian, Indian, Pakistan candidates, and last but not least are candidates from Bangladesh. People from Asian countries can imagine working at the same time as studying, making it even more tough, especially for people with a family trying to get their Fellowship. But to progress in the medical profession, this degree is a must. This was only my third attempt at the final examination. In this examination we can take as much time as we like. It is held at four places: London, Edinburgh, Glasgow and Dublin. The Fellowship Degree is counted as the same, it is not easy to get. One mistake means you must book your place for next examination. It has happened with me. Pass in four and fail in the fifth. No consideration for the next examination, you therefore fail in all. It happened to me once when I failed only at one place. When the result came, I did not know, whilst holding the result in my hand, whether to celebrate, cry or break my head against wall. These things are not uncommon.

I remember one of my friends working in the Surgery Department, a middle-aged Muslim fellow from Pakistan. Once I went to his house on invitation. I was introduced to the family immediately, perhaps they liked me and told me "Everything is good. We are all living quite well. Children doing well in school, but the big problem is this Fellowship for my husband". My friends wife told me he had taken the examination at different places but the result was negative all the time. "It has gone to everybody's head, this examination that when my children go to Musjid to pray, they only pray Allah, please give Fellowship Degree to our father." This was my third attempt. I was taking my final examination for the Fellowship in Edinburgh. It is a well-known university in the world of doctors. It is second in preference only to London. When I finished my examination again my intuitions came back to me, telling me I passed the exam before I received the official result.

I was taking a shower early in the morning. There was a big bang on my door of the shower. I said, "Please wait, I will finish soon."

My Junior Doctor said, "Anish, come out, there is a letter for you." I came out, picked up the letter which was already open. My Junior Doctor, also a friend of mine, was hiding behind the door, watching. I read the letter. Again, it was like when I stood first in the Delhi University in 1969. This time, it was December 1985, and the same response of my body as if nothing was moving, no breathing for some time, only standing. My Junior Doctor friend came and seeing me standing still, hugged me so much that we both fell on the ground. Next, I remember we were both hugging each other, dancing in the corridor.

All the other residents came out, "What has happened?" When they knew I had got the Fellowship of Royal College of Surgeons,

Edinburgh, everybody on the floor joined and congratulated me. The news spread in the hospital like wildfire.

This celebration is right, and why not - one of their hospital doctors achieving the biggest degree from the Royal College of Surgeons, Edinburgh? At that time, I remembered my father and said to myself "You should have waited for this for some more time, but I know you would have died telling all other people in India bout this." Everybody tried to make me realise what I had achieved and it did not sink in straight away, but gradually. Then I also changed with time. I knew my biggest achievements were this Royal College of Surgeons Fellow, Edinburgh and at the age of eighteen, my name on the merit board at Delhi University in 1969. But on top of everyone's achievement I had my family now. My younger daughter, only twenty-seven years old who is banking in central London; my son, only twenty nine, is also a Fellow of the Royal College getting trained in Central London at a top hospital to become a Consultant in Orthopaedics. But, above all, my wife, whose sixty-first birthday is soon, in a few days. When I see her, she looks the same to me as when I married her years ago. I don't remember any change in her beauty with age. All my old friends say this as well.

Now, with one chapter finished I will start the next one with my family. For this I had to find a girl first.

Before I go into this, I want to write about my liking for alcohol. I believe this is one gene in my chromosomes in the cells in my body. All these genes, as we know, are different. That is why I liked alcohol instead of drugs, smoking, gambling, ketamine, aggressive behaviour or abnormality from birth. I think I have a gene for liking alcohol. I noticed this when I first tasted alcohol in the form of beer. To start with, this half a bottle of beer was very enjoyable to me, and with regular intake my body got used to this. Now, one bottle of good whisky is the same as the effect of half a bottle of beer when I started at the age of 25 because before this age, I did not have money to spend on alcohol. Once I started earning, my first priority was the intake of alcohol for enjoyment. I have been drinking for the last forty years. I have cut down my drinking now. I don't know. I now drink only four days in a month but when I drink, once I open a bottle, I won't stop until I see the bottom of it. Forty years of drinking. To me it is similar to how smoking causes cancer, but even a non-smoker can get lung cancer. Same with the alcohol. The intake of alcohol is quite different from the drug once you get a liking for the drug. It is very difficult to come out of it despite any treatment given, the patient reverts back to their source of enjoyment. As I mentioned, I liked this drug because it had a totally different effect. I spoke to one doctor who admitted to me that he was getting treatment for drug intake. I was there in the best Indian Rehabilitation Centre, forced by my niece who was working as a Consultant in Anaesthesia in India. I never wanted to get admitted but I was forced.

I spoke to another doctor admitted for rehabilitation due to drug intake. I became friendly with him being as we were the only two doctors in the same ward. He used to discuss everything with me. I also met his parent, a very nice family, and he was the only son. The father was running his own practice and owned big nursing home in Haryana, and his son was a drug addict. They were so upset that the mother cried in front of me and said, "Look, we have everything, why has God done this to us, such a nice looking young boy who is a doctor and a drug addict." I consoled them from my side as I was very senior and retired at the time and I suggested once he gets out of the rehabilitation centre. Don't leave him alone, make sure somebody is with him always. The effect of the drug was given in books as well.

The effect after drug intake is like a hallucination effect. I had this effect with alcohol only once, the same as the other doctor described. I got this effect after consuming too much alcohol every day for quite a few days continuously. It was too good to describe. I saw some of the movie characters when I looked outside the window and was flying in paradise surrounded by everything, clouds, rain, snow, hanging gardens, birds, animals, the way some would like to be forever – this is the effect my friend the drug addict described. Now you can imagine why they don't leave and live without this, no matter what you give them as treatment. They will go back to drug intake. As I mentioned, I tried acupuncture needles in my ears in the rehabilitation centre, tablets to prevent intake of alcohol, isolation and drugs they give to prevent drinking. The side effect one gets is stated to be: sickness, red face, uneasiness and nausea. Despit all this, in the best rehabilitation centre near Delhi, everything was available smuggled from outside. Smoking, alcohol, drugs, anything, pay the extra cash and get delivery at your bed with so many security people around you. I saw all this myself. In other words, it was like a mini underground business. All good things happen. I even saw during my one month stay, fighting to take dominance like an action movie. I saw, in front of me, it was like watching a real-life movie. I felt how lucky I am to see this real-life movie happening and the director, I believe, in this case was my God watching everything. I don't know if his reaction would be laughing or crying. In this top rehabilitation institute, I saw it all happening every day.

As I mentioned, nothing works. If some are cured, it is with the person himself like me, but I was never addicted, never convicted approaching seventy years of my age. Never drunk, in life. But I want to make it clear, I have not read in any book the definition of drunk. I believe a person with alcohol intake gets a complete loss of senses, but I am not sure. I never reached this stage. I was lucky to once have the experience of hallucination, that too from drinking alone in my room excessively. If one decides to cut down or stop totally it must be the person himself, otherwise no treatment is effective, just a waste of money and manpower.

I believe as a person, alcohol is a gift from God, at least for me. I have used alcohol for all purposes of enjoyment. If I wanted to sleep after reading before taking an examination, for so many hours when my mind, head and brain was blocked, I found it a waste of time to be in front of a book without anything going into my head, all useless, I just used to drink and sleep. Whenever drinks were available for a ceremony, bad things happened to me. Alcohol has always been my friend. As I mentioned in my life: myself, God, books and alcohol. I love all of them. Everyone knows now that I like or love alcohol. I don't mind this; it is a fact. But I never misused.

I never got convicted for anything after taking alcohol. I am healthy for a seventy-year-old. My profession is like going to temple: hospital and temple, my home, they are same. I worship all of them. I don't remember any incident after the intake of alcohol because most of the time I like to drink alone, especially now at this age. Alcohol was always my friend, like a good friend. I would prefer to be like this if God permits me. As everybody knows, I like my friend called alcohol. So many times, the shopkeepers asked me what bottle I wanted and they say "Doc, don't worry, take it, give us the money when you have it."

So many times I refused but at times I get embarrassed. And to please me and perhaps him, I take it and give money. Then I never go to that shop until I have money. So many close friends of mine used to send messages to me to have a few drinks with me, back in India. You can imagine, a young man known not only because my name is written on the Delhi University merit board but also the alcohol, or perhaps both. How does one do both of these things?

I must say, one thing, sex after intake of alcohol is much more enjoyable. Even my wife said this once.

People keep asking me, "You have all the qualities, no blemish, why do you drink so much?" I said "Because I like it." My present GP who is very good in Amersham, UK asked me the same question. I said "Because I like it." He said that is fair enough then. You keep on doing what you are doing. He did not say go and drink more, because he is an English trained doctor. He said, all your tests are normal and now you have also cut down your drink. Just maintain everything, take regular drugs as prescribed to you and regular food intake, all meals in a balanced diet as recommended.

My brother told me once that with the money I have spent on alcohol, we could have bought another house in India. I told my brother that when I was on my holidays from the UK in India, my friend requested me to tell my colleague not to be so miserly – what is he going to do with saved money? My friend said his explanation is to enjoy the best retired doctor life. This miser doctor died only a few days before his retirement. I told my brother, you understand now why I live my life the way I want to. My brother and I were not so lucky in childhood, always living hand to mouth. Now, when we have something with us, why not enjoy it? My brother had no answer to give. I knew he is thinking of himself. Both my brother and his wife are earning. I gave money to all my relations whenever they demanded it. They knew as everybody knew that I was working in Saudi Arabia as a private Consultant Surgeon doctor. They applied all the methods to snatch money from me. They took away money which I used to send to my father. They would not leave that money either. My sister told me about this. Be careful of your money to your father. My elder brother would take from him with some sort of excuse. Then I started sending money to my married second eldest sister. She used to give money to him every month. When my father died, my sister called me separately. She said you now have left over money which you used to send to your father. I could not believe it but only look up to God and ask "Do I have to see this also in my life?" My sister immediately noticed this and said, don't worry, he is still watching you. I am sure he must be giving blessings to you, now I am going to have another new life. I suppose it's my third birth. I never wanted to get married because I lost my hair at a young age. But Hindu religion tells us God wishes not to end life without having a family.

I used to be very good looking in my childhood as I mentioned. I used to get scared to go for my haircut. My sister once told me, run away from home and join the film industry. When I was young and lost my hair, they said, which I believe, that there is always another way. I started using a wig. Again, what can I write? Some good physical appearance but this time I ignored everything and carried on with my life the way I like, because up until now, I had learned quite a lot and matured myself and as I am growing more and I am gaining more with my age.

So, to start a family, I had to find a girl. I did not get married before because I wanted to get my Fellowship of Royal College to have better status. To have a better chance to get the girl of my choice. I also wanted to have a house before marriage in the UK so that the girl who normally comes from very good Indian families should not repent their decision to come to the UK – at least give them whatever to them make them comfortable, if not better.

As I mentioned, the girl I was looking for, I already had in my mind. I had so many proposals before marriage, both medical, non-medical, known to the family, the relations and daughters.

They say marriages are made in heaven but celebrated on earth. I know this is the case with me. But I had a girl in my mind. When I was medical student doing my studies in Medical College to become a doctor, I used to see one of the Consultant Surgeons, Plastic Surgeon, one's wife. She, along with her friend of the same age, used to go around our playground in front of our doctor's student residence. Every day, I used to see her with someone I desire. I was so young at that time, nobody could guess I had this in me, I would like to have my wife like this. She used to be an air hostess before marriage. Slim, trim, tall, good looking, perfect for high class society.

I thought about this, now the time has come. The best place for me to find a wife is to go back to my homeland, India, and give a proper advertisement in the matrimonial column in my hometown newspaper. I mentioned before about my intuition power. I had planned everything but before starting, I knew, asking myself, I am going to Delhi and was the mission going to be a successful one? I knew the answer already. I booked my flight with all the plans for me. Now a Dr, not a Mr, is going to India to find a girl for marriage. No more worrying about any examinations. I boarded the plane for a brand new life – to start my life to become a doctor, then again the drama to start my life in the UK. Now I was going to face another one, but if this was to happen so soon I did not know.

I was lucky to have another sibling next to me, an Indian with typical Indian clothes, like Mahatma Gandhi used to wear in India. An air hostesses came to ask about drinks. The fellow next to myself asked for an orange juice. But, for me, a double dose of scotch on the rocks, it was celebration time, I passed my Fellowship and was a new doctor. Within a few minutes, both of us became friendly. It was only seventy minutes in the air. I had my drinks and was looking to ask for my second one. The announcement suddenly came on the speaker in the plane. Within a few minutes we were landing. "Please fasten your seatbelt." Immediately, my alcohol intake gave me the signal. I looked at my watch and asked my nearby sitting friend the time. I made sure it was only seventy minutes of plane in air. My friend in the seat next to me asked, has Delhi come? I laughed to myself.

He asked me, I had to reply and be honest. I said, "I think there is some problem, we are not landing at Delhi but at Heathrow Airport." He asked what the problem was, I said, "it may be bomb threat". Without speaking to anyone, all the air hostesses started running around, all the faces of the crew were very worried. Being a doctor, I immediately read what was happening. I was so lucky to have my double scotch whisky from the start. I saw my friend take out our Hindu Holy Book and he started reciting loudly. I told him, "Very good, now this plane won't blow up. Please pray for me also because I am going to start my new family."

Eventually, the plane landed at Heathrow, all around us were flashing lights, moving vehicles, the fire brigade, ambulances, police vehicles. It was difficult to count the number, it was as if the whole airport was under seige.

When the plane landed just a few minutes were given to the passengers to take off their shoes. "Don't carry any bags. All doors including the exit door will open automatically. From the exit door, a sheet will go down. Please, go onto landing calmly, go to exit door and slide down on the sliding sheet. If you sustained any friction injury, it will be handled immediately at ground." I took off my shoes but I did not leave my bag because my things were in there, including my medicine as I had drunk also. I went down the plane on slide. I took it as fun. When we were standing away from the plane, in case the plane caught fire, one Indian lady passenger came to me. I don't know what her profession was but one of the passengers asked me, "Did you experience anything like this before." I said "No, this is my first one." She said, "Good, you are doing very well." I said, "I am."

All the passengers were now in the main hall of the Heathrow Airport. The next flight will leave for Delhi in one day. During this time, all the passengers were given the option to either to stay in one of the arranged hotels by the airline or they could go to their own residence in London and spend one day at home and board the flight again. Instead of living in London, why leave this opportunity to stay in a Five Star Central London hotel? I opted for staying at hotel. Again, it was party time for whole day. I enjoyed the Central London hotel at the expense of the airline because of the hoax call of a bomb scare. After one day, again I boarded the flight from Heathrow

Alcoholic Doctor

to Delhi. I had one of the best flights experiences because the crew was very generous to the passengers because of the rough time they had the night before.

I landed safely in Delhi Airport. Now it was action time. First things first, I had to put an advertisement in the Delhi newspaper. A London-based doctor wants to get married to an Indian girl. From the next day, the phone never stopped ringing. The first to come to my home to discuss with my family about the ad regarding marriage was a Major-General. He came with his wife. From the first day, we arranged for a private car to go to see the girl regarding my ad with the intention of future marriage. From the day I arrived in Delhi on my holiday from London hospital, we used to go every day to see desired girls at the family's request. Sometimes, the girl's family used to come first to my home without their daughter. That is quite acceptable because of the Indian culture. As we know, I have written that marriages are arranged in heaven, in my case, as I have written before. My intuition already had told me, go to Delhi for the mission but enjoy this as a holiday.

That is what I did. I don't know how many girls I saw. Even the taxi driver said one day, "What sort of girl you are looking for?" I did not reply, but I knew what sort. I don't remember how many girls I saw on that trip. I decided to come back to London. Before coming back, my eldest sister said, "So our innocent youngest family brother is going back alone." I said, "Don't worry sister, I will marry only the one who is waiting for me."

I came back and started working again in the same hospital. To my surprise, within a week, I received three or four phone calls from families interested to introduce me to their daughter. I asked, "Who gave you the information that I am looking for a girl to get married?" He said from India, his relation phoned him in England regarding the matrimonial advertisement in the Delhi newspaper. Out of the three, two of the girls were working as an air hostess, one was settled in the UK and the other was here on holidays - an Indian air hostess, staying with her brother, a resident of London but originally from India Punjab. The rest of the family was still in India, she was an Indian resident.

I happened to see all three out of them and I liked the one from India the most. I phoned, my present wife and we both agreed on a deal basis. I was introduced to the girl's family and their known relations. All the relations I met, I knew they are alright or good.

My marriage took place in a Sikh Temple. My religion is Hindu and the girl was a Sikh, myself from Delhi and the girl, my wife, from Punjab in India. It was a very simple marriage in a Gurdwara in Central London, my friend, my brother and my nephew came from India to attend my marriage. The registrar marriage was performed before the Indian marriage ceremony. Just imagine the girl's mother and father did not come to attend the marriage. Otherwise, they attended all the marriages. I still now have not found any answer as to why they weren't there. One of the relatives said they wanted to save money to spend on their daughter's marriage. But I told them, marriage was done as a deal.

I finished my job as Orthopaedic registrar in Central London and I was lucky to get a job in Saudi Arabia as a Consultant in one of the big hospitals of the Saudi Government. My friends came to know and they said very good. I, with my only son at the time of my appointment, left with my wife for the job in Saudi Arabia with my wife.

Now my fourth life starts from when I arrive at Riyadh Airport from London. My first life began when I got awareness of this universe. My second life started on arrival in the UK. My third was after my marriage and now I had a new fourth life.

I landed at Riyadh Airport in the evening. It is a unique place. Pin drop silence. There were so many people standing in rows to show their entry visas to the men at the desks, each separate in a line. All with different types of nationality. I showed my passport with the entry visa, which I got from UK Saudi Embassy. Within a minute, I walked in to have a final security check before entry into Saudi Arabia. I had nothing, apart from my clothes I was wearing and I carried one picture of my favourite Indian Gods and a statue of Shiva, our God. The security officer said, "You are not allowed to carry your God in Saudi Arabia." I said, "What should I do?" He said, "Just leave picture with us." I did not dare to ask any questions.

I asked about the statue. I was sure he did not understand the value of the brass metal statue of Shiva, our God. He said, "You can take this with you." I knew he did not know about Shiva and he thought it was one of the decorations from India. I thanked God. At least he has given one God of India to take with me. I quietly put the statue in my case. My intuition came to me while I was standing in the row for the passport check. I was going to do a Consultant Orthopaedic job for one year. At the airport, my intuition told me that I was going to live there for exactly twelve years. This proved later to be absolutely right. After twelve years, I resigned from the hospital because of my children's education. I had to leave because there was no English school for foreigners with children above the age of fourteen.

Next, now, the time of truth had come. My new job was at a place away from the Riyadh hospital, near the Yemen border, a place called Najran. It was a small place. When I arrived alone in Najran, while going to the hospital, I noticed that the whole town was decorated and lit with small lights everywhere. I asked the driver if this was normal? "Do they switch on these lights every day?" He said, "No, this has been going on for two weeks. The King of Saudi Arabia, King Fahd, is expected to visit the city of Najran for the first time." I said, "Oh, really?" I thought it was normal because of the oil money. I was sure not of my presence.

I started my job of one year in the hospital and people around me immediately recognised my work. My job got automatically extended for another year. After three months, as per the Saudi rules, my family joined me. At the beginning, one has to join a hospital alone according to the rules. Then, after three months, if you survive the initial stage then your family can join you. I was working with a very Senior Orthopaedics Consultant, a Fellow of Royal College of Surgeons from the UK and some junior doctors working in the Orthopaedics Department. My Senior Orthopaedics Consultant was so scared to operate he hardly came to the operating theatre to operate. He probably was aware of the Saudi Sharia laws. Any minor mistake is then known to everyone. Any major mistake, then the only one to save you is God or the King of Saudi Arabia, otherwise your fate is written on the wall. Because I was so young that to from the UK as a new Orthopaedic Consultant, I was full of energy. Whatever I had learnt I started doing in Saudi Arabia. I am sure nobody had seen so many operations being performed within one year in that hospital. The administration and staff immediately came to know about it.

The one case I remember was when I started treating children with hip problems, CDH, congenital dysplastic hips, unstable or dislocated hips. Depending on the case, it can be treated as required, both operatively and non-operatively with the help of orthopaedic books. I learnt all the techniques to handle these cases. The administration was fully aware of this too. They were quite pleased because now all these types of cases were getting treatment at their own hospital. Patients didn't only come from Najran city, but people got the news from surrounding areas and they started coming too. My workload increased so much because my Senior Orthopaedic Consultant did not want to treat most of the cases because of his fear of making a mistake in Saudi Arabia. With each good result of surgery and treatment, my confidence grew. At the end of my two-year contract, I had handled all types of congenital dysplastic hips in children on my own.

As my experience grew, I started operating on children of up to the age of ten. I operated on ten year old dyslplastic hips too. I still remember that the old experienced Orthopaedic Surgeon would not think to operate. He would plan to operate a few months before touching the patient. I had only seen one case that I remember of ten-year-old dysplastic operation done in a periphery big hospital in the UK. This too was done by an Indian Senior Surgeon. I was present in the theatre. It was my first Orthopaedic job as a Junior Doctor, thirty-five years ago now. I did not understand much about Orthopaedics then. I asked the nurse, "What did he do?" The nurse said, "Nobody knows what he did, only one person knows that and that's himself." This Consultant looking at my body language, he said to me, "Keep dreaming, keep dreaming." I knew what he was saying and I said nothing at that time.

I wish I could meet him now to tell him about my dreams and what I have achieved. I don't know if he's still alive or not. Anyway,

I leave that to God. Professionally, apart from achieving an FRCS Degree from Edinburgh, this was the most productive period of my life from a professionalism point and also financially. The best thing was that was nothing to spend your money on. In Najran there was no drinking or gambling. Local travel has no problem as the petrol price was cheaper than water. Even the accommodation was free. There were no theatres and no tourist areas around. God was very kind to me because it was the perfect time to come to Saudi Arabia when my family was young. A young growing family with private security and with money flowing in.

I remember an incident after one year in Saudi when I had some money in the bank. I decided to visit my family in India. My wife said while you are in India, I will go with our young son to England to meet her family. We agreed on this with good mutual consent. I booked the flight from Riyadh to Delhi travelling alone. I was lucky again as my co-passenger on the seat next to me was an educated Saudi and could converse with me in English. We had a discussion on so many subjects. He was quite interested in alcoholic drinks available in the UK. We became quite friendly on the flight. This is normal when two people have got the same thinking and are on the same wavelength. At the time of departure, before landing at Indira Gandhi Airport in Delhi, this Saudi friend of mine asked for two bottles of Scotch Whisky. I was happy, at least he will have a good time in India for some days. When the air hostess gave him the bottles, he paid the bill. He said, "Doc, one for you, one for me." I said, "Please don't do this." He said, "Come on, Doc, you are my friend now and you are working as a doctor in Saudi, maybe I'll be your patient one day. I am giving you an example of how nice the Saudi people are. If they like you, they have faith in you. If they don't like you, one knows the result himself."

This was not the first gift from that I received from a local Saudi. I used to get so many watches from patients and their families and when they came to know I have a young family, my son and now daughter, they started giving me small gold jewellery for my children. One day, I did feel that it was getting too much. I went to the Chief of the hospital and I told him about these watches and gold chain gifts I received from Saudi patients. I said, "I don't want them, what should I do?" He said, "Doctor, I know and the whole hospital knows about this." He said, "Those Saudi people are sensitive. If you say no to the innocent villagers, they will get hurt. Don't say no, take the gifts and come and deposit them here with my office secretary. I will inform them. They will take care of it." I was so happy and started giving back the gifts given to me to the Head Saudi Office Administrator of the hospital.

As I wrote about nice people, everybody is nice if you are nice. Even the baddie can behave in a nice way if you are nice to them. Sometimes, body language is all you need, and it does its job with one's involvement. Some people's presence is all that is required when the time is right.

I suffered in my life because of my truthfulness. This I will never give up whatever the cost.

Since marriage and even after marriage, and on our honeymoon, my wife started saying, "I will leave you and go away." Now more than thirty years later, she is still with me as a result of my honesty.

I was lucky to see a sandstorm in Saudi Arabia which is a totally unique natural event. Suddenly, the whole sky gets full of dust. Dust starts falling down everywhere, along with large stones falling from the sky. All the traffic stops suddenly and when the storm finishes, everything goes back to normal. In my twelve years in Saudi Arabia, I was lucky to see it happen only once. I am glad that at least I saw it once in my life. People talk about tornados, what about sandstorms?

Saudi people are very humble and nice. They are very good people if they like the person. If you commit a mistake then you must face punishment according to their law, Sharia Law. I happened to see two decapitations done. This act is performed openly in front of the general public with people of all ages, old people and young children, are there to witness it. The act of decapitation is done in a totally professional way. They are masters as they have been doing it for years. The person who does the decapitation is also a professional. The job runs in the family, passed from one generation to another normally. There is no footage of it, nobody is taking photos there. I did not see any cameras around. The act is performed in front of the Mosque after the afternoon prayer on a Friday.

Before the act of decapitation, everyone gathers around a solid cement big square in front of the Mosque, the size of a small football ground. Everyone stands watching at the periphery. Then the procedure begins. The ambulance and fire brigade are already present on the side, slightly away from the decapitation. Vehicles come slowly one by one when they are allowed to. The vehicle has completely covered windows. Then the guards come out with big guns in their hands and start taking position in the square, starting from the periphery, standing in squares. They stand in rows with small distance between them. The main centre space is left for the final van to come through with the culprit and some guards.

Before the final vehicle comes into the centre, a vehicle comes with a massive African man with a big sword around his waist and some guards. They freely take place in the centre where they would like to be, and the big man with the sword also walks with ease, chatting with guards. Then the last vehicle comes through. Silence is everywhere. Guards come out first, followed by the prisoner to be decapitated and then more guards follow. The culprit is highly sedated, walking with their hands and legs tied. Everyone takes their position. The culprit gets put in position, the big man comes to the same spot for final act. He draws his sword which shines with the reflection of the bright sun. He raises the sword as high as he can and with both his hands and in one stroke, hits the back of the neck at his chosen point.

Bright red blood rushes out from the big vessels of the neck, and with slight movements of the limbs, the man falls down. A vehicle arrives quickly to take the body away followed by another vehicle to clean up the area, followed by the last vehicle to wash the place so it is left totally clean, ready for next act whenever required.

Immediately, all the spectators disperse very quickly as if nothing had happened. In the same way, an act is performed to chop off the hand clean off the wrist of thieves. In this case, after the chopping of the hand, it is thrown up in the air. But this is what I have been told, I have not seen it myself. This is done so that the public can see the punishment of crime.

I was lucky in my first job, as I was the main Orthopaedic Surgeon operating. I was promoted to Chief of the Orthopaedic Department when I was not even forty years of age. My old Consultant left after one year and was replaced by another old one who was no better. I operated on one VIP Saudi patient. He invited me to his farm which was a very well-planned farm with all sorts of animals. The Sheikh had all sorts of exotic birds and animals. There was a small man-made lake created by a specialist from Europe with natural flora and fauna. It really was a grand day with local music, singing, dancing, it was a treat to watch. I felt so lucky to be invited. At the end, a gift was given to me by the patient's relative for my work. The one thing they are proud of is their dates, which is specially grown on their farms, camel milk and water melons. The whole generation survived on these things. Petrol was discovered too but much later on.

Regarding beauty, their Royalty was the most beautiful. I was also lucky when I was invited to one of the sheikh's farms. There was a blue sheep, white and blue, I had never seen anything like it. There were also white tigers which I had seen in zoos but I had never seen a blue sheep anywhere. He, the sheikh, cared for the blue sheep more than his children.

I also learnt about the Arabian aphrodisiac, which they grow in soil like ginger and dig it out to find the roots which is used like Viagra. The Arabians are crazy about sex. My Arabian friend told me that on Friday they all must have sex. On Fridays there is nothing else on their mind but one thing which they must satisfy.

Because of my work in Orthopaedics in Saudi Arabia, before the end of my contract, there was a formal prize distribution ceremony. I was awarded a Saudi prize and Merit Certificate from the Saudi Government. I was always chosen to go on conferences paid for fully by Saudis – the travel, accommodation and conference expenses. I was sent to Davos in Switzerland four times, once to Orlando in the US and once to New York by the Saudi Government. I am grateful to them. To go to these countries is best when you are young with a young family. Higher education forced me to come back to the UK for my children. I could either stay or send the children to boarding school in a country like the UK. I made the decision, which everybody agreed with, to return to UK with my family.

My son is currently getting training in Guys Hospital in the UK, to become an Orthopaedic Consultant. He is thirty years old, already he is a Fellow of the Royal College of Surgeons. Sometimes my friends from Medical College practising in UK tease me saying, "You went to a school, where you used to get training sitting on the floor. Look at your son. If you had this training, God knows what you would have achieved." That is also what my eldest brother told me also before he died. He was a very good scientist and also received awards from the Indian Government for his work in husbandry, the science of milk production.

Another incident I remember; I mentioned that I belonged to a middle class family. I never have any sort of luxury, not even proper clothes, my best clothes were my uniform.

In the UK, before going to Saudi I lived in the same way. I just managed to live comfortably. All of my salary from the hospital went towards the mortgage. I managed to survive comfortably but only after doing extra time. My whole life was transformed, when I started work in Saudi Arabia. The accommodation was free, my children's education was free and everything else was cheap. At the end of the year an extra half month's salary was paid into my bank account.

I never had any toys when I was young. I had it in my mind that whenever I had money, I would try to give to my children what I didn't have. When I started working in my first hospital, I was doing very well. My name came up in Saudi Newspaper a number of times. With money in the bank, I used to take my very small children to a toy shop. One day, the Saudi shop owner called me over. He said, "Doc, can I have word with you?" I said, "Yes, what can I do for you?" He said, it is not what I can for him, but what he could do for me. "Listen, we all know you are from England and originally from India, everybody knows you are very good. Everyone loves their children. I have a big toy shop of my own. I have small children but that does not mean that I should give them a new toy every day." He said, "Do you think I can't afford it?" I got the message. He said, "Please don't spoil them. Love them, but don't spoil. Show love by not throwing away your money. Look, you are here in this desert far away from your own people, please don't do it." After that day, I was careful but not that strict.

Money started coming in gradually which I enjoyed to the maximum. I had a great life, holidays, liquor, good food and shopping. Money was coming in so quickly that I started playing with properties. I got the experience to buy land, a house and a farm in Delhi. With experience, I came to know things regarding properties. The most profitable opportunities could also be the most dangerous, it can even destroy you. If you are lucky you must be at right place at the right time to buy property. The most important thing is to always be present to take care of the property as if you are selling the property, otherwise it can be a big gamble. If it goes wrong, then there is no comeback. It can be bad for one's self but worse for the family. I have gone through it all but with grace of God, I have had good luck.

My grown-up children say that they are now adults. My daughter is a banker and is married to a young engineer in the UK, they both live in their own house in Central London. My children still at times tease me, "Pa you were so soft from the beginning. Whenever we wanted anything, we always used to come to you. Mum was good but strict, not like you." If we used to go to any shop, and if I could afford it I would say just three words to the shopkeeper, "Pack it up." My grown-up children say that because I spoiled them, they got the same habit now and tell the shopkeeper the same thing. I say, "I don't know whether I did right or wrong. I wanted to give you everything which I did not get in my childhood."

It is true that I spoiled my children but at the same time, I gave them the best education. My son is on course to become an Orthopaedic Consultant. My daughter is an investment banker, now working in a German bank in London. I have no regrets about anything. Regarding spoiling my children when in Saudi Arabia we used to travel to different countries on holiday. Everybody was excited to go away. My wife to save money, booked one three-star hotel. We stayed in the hotel for one night. The next day, we were going out in the evening. My son walking behind me and my daughter a little behind him, followed by my wife. We intended to have nice dinner by the seaside and were walking to the local restaurant. I knew something was wrong. My son said in a very polite way, "Do you call this a holiday?" I asked, "Why? It's a nice hotel, nice place, what is the problem? You like this hotel?" He said, "Me and my sister, we both don't like this at all." Looking at their faces, I said, "Don't worry, your mother booked it." The next morning, I called a taxi. Luckily, we got a place in one of the best five-star hotels on the beach.

Both my children came to me and hugged me. My wife was smiling and looking at what was happening. They said "Thanks, this is what we call a holiday." But this is the problem: once you spoil them, there is no coming back. Everybody who is earning a lot of money and managing it on their own, the way they want, is happy. You have to take care of it yourself but you want to get whatever is money can buy. You earned it. Now you have to manage it yourself. Who told you you'd earn a life like this? I don't want to enjoy when I am old. When one is old, you only survive on the medicine you take and can manage. The body gradually allows all the organs to wear and tear until they are replaced and completely stop working. That means the end.

There is no doubt, you should enjoy every day all you want to, but it is like this – I feel maximum enjoyment is properly done when you are young and have money, not overdoing anything. That is why we all remember our childhood, school, mates, colleges. In old age, it is very difficult to make friends. You are lucky if an arranged marriage works for you in older age. Memories of school and college will always be the best memories.

When I sit and compare my holidays in school, college or in old age, holidays in college days always remain the best, whether I had enough money or not. In those days, even with less money I used to manage somehow with friends whether they were alive or had already left to look for their new life. The rules and regulations in Saudi Arabia stated in order to change workplace one had to come back to the place of hire and then go back. In my case, I have never had to go back to my original place of work. I went straight from one hospital to another in Saudi Arabia. I joined the next hospital in Saudi for one year. It was Bisha near Mecca Medina, forty five miles drive from my hospital working place.

I am a religious man, but because I am Hindu, I was not allowed to worship there. I am told by my colleagues from working at that time that the atmosphere is totally different around worship in the place of a Muslim. They say it is the best place and the only place with air conditioning. There is a unique atmosphere there. That is why Allah God has made this place for him, for the Muslims to come and visit him in this place. Even from the outside, I could feel the difference. Even if I was not allowed to go near his place, I would have liked to go.

One year passed of me working there and the only other thing I remember is the Shawarma, a Saudi local sandwich which had bread, flamed cooked meat with a little sauce. In Saudi, I only liked this food. So good and very cheap. With less than a pound's worth, one can fill his tummy. My children, now grown up, still remember and miss it – the shawarma we get in London is nowhere near the original one from Saudi. In fact, my children left Saudi more than fifteen years ago yet they still remember their life there. Still sometimes they say, "Pa, when can we visit Saudi Arabia again?" I told them that this is not a tourist place. If you go on your own, it can be a problem as it is not even that safe when you are working there. While visiting, I remember my first hospital. My hospital administrator was an English guy that became friendly with me because he was also from London, UK and because of the good hospital work I did.

One day, he said, Anish, "What happened yesterday?" I asked, "What?" He said, "I went around the roundabout in my car and one of the Saudi's hit my car from behind. We both stopped on the side of the site of accident. The police came and I said this is totally the Saudi's fault. The policeman told me "No, it was your fault totally" I said, "My God, this accident is in front of you, I am telling you what happened." The person who hit the car was also present. The policeman told me "This is your fault because, why are you here? Who told you to come here? This is not a tourist place." The policeman gave him a slip of the accident and ordered me to pay for the repair of his car. Luckily the Saudi man was very good. He said, don't worry, he will repair it himself." I said to the English administrator that I think the policeman is right. Who told us to come here, apart from the reason called money? The administrator said, "Kurar, I think you are right. I just came back, my car is in the garage for repair now."

I said, "Very sensible, man, no point in arguing anyway as you are not going to win, the choice is yours."

By now, I had gotten used to Saudi Arabia. My family was also very happy to be in Saudi. My children were going to a private English school and I felt like a resident of three countries now, India, UK and Saudi Arabia. I finished my job in Bisha, near Mecca. My next job was in Hafar-Al-Betan, a military hospital near the Iraqi border. The border was the one which the Iraqis used to try and enter Saudi Arabia during Kuwait/Iraq War. This did not end well for Kuwait but had no effect for Saudi Arabia because of the Americans, who had too much involvement.

I joined this new hospital. As before, it was a direct appointment from one hospital to another Saudi Arabia hospital without me going back to London, my place of hire. Once again their own rule of me having to come back to London if joining a new hospital would be overruled. In joining a new hospital I had a little argument in front of the second in command, because the Number One Chief was on holiday, the Brigadier, and I knew this is going to hit back at me. I kept on doing my routine work. As we know, one mistake in Saudi Arabia means a ticket in hand for a flight back to your place of hire. Your luggage would automatically reach the airport before departure.

After eight months of working in the hospital, I received a letter that my services are no longer required in this military Saudi hospital. I went to see the Brigadier-Chief of the hospital. It was morning time and they knew beforehand that I was going to come and see the Chief. Both Brigadier number one and his number two in command were present in the room. I already knew what the issue was and why I got this this letter without any notice. I said to both of them, "I am sorry if I have upset anybody, did I do anything wrong?" Brigadier said "No you have not done anything wrong. For the last eight months, we wanted to sack you. But we could not find any fault. We wanted to sack you so we have done that." I said, "I am sorry if I upset anybody." They knew what I meant. They said, "Alright you go and work" so I thanked them.

I worked normally and finished my job which then got extended automatically from one year to two years. I finished two years. I got another job, this time for one year in one of the private hospitals in Riyadh, the capital of Saudi Arabia. I enjoyed this one year, then finished this job. After this job, I was lucky to have another job in the best hospital in Riyadh, the capital of Saudi Arabia. It was a very big hospital and a referral hospital for treatment of difficult cases that are unable to have treatment at their own local hospitals. During this interval period of six months, before joining the next job in Saudi Arabia I decided to go to Delhi and work as Consultant Orthopaedic in a private hospital in Delhi.

This period of six months was quite relaxing and enjoyable. Working after three months, I was doing well but I found no point in carrying on with the job in Delhi.

I decided there was no point in carrying on with the job because my expenditure was more than my earnings. The rent of the place in a posh area was too much. 50,000 rupees per month plus spending money for lavish living. I decided to shift to Hill Station and was there for three months. I rented a big house of my own with money spent on only one seventh of what I was spending in Delhi on a rented flat. Moreover, the famous Hill Station of India was only a half an hour journey from my place of living, called Dehradun, and the tourist Hill Station place called Mussoorie in India. Three months passed then another relaxing holiday, good living, food, drinks, servants and dogs. I bought two small dogs, one a German Shephard, the other a Pomeranian. Before re-joining the Riyadh job, I gave both dogs to my friend in Dehradun who wanted to have them.

Accidentally, out of fascination, I bought a one-acre piece of big land to build a nice big house with a big garden all around. There were thirty-five Litchi trees. However, I sold the land later. The most attractive fascination was nearby, Hill Station and the Litchi trees on my land on the famous main road of Dehradun, India. When the Litchi trees have the fruits in summer seasons, it looks like the green big trees are loaded with decorated red medium size bulbs, a real treat.

After three months I was ready to go back to action to do a final job in Riyadh. It was the best hospital in Riyadh to get admitted for treatment. They can arrange any specialist consultant from abroad in no time. Otherwise, most of the Royals get treatment from abroad. I was lucky to get job in this hospital. This is mainly a referral hospital but locals also get treatment here in my Orthopaedic Department.

There were sub-specialities of Child Paediatrics, an Orthopaedic Department, tumour treatment and joint replacement, trauma spine surgery and the Orthopaedic Department. All these subspecialist units had their own Consultant with one main Head of the Department Consultant. All these Consultants were from America or Europe. My job was as an Assistant Consultant. It is more relaxing than a Consultant because it has less responsibility. During my stay in this hospital of more than five years, I remember only two incidents. My job was a rotational job working in each sub-speciality of the Orthopaedic Department. This time, I was working in the Tumour Orthopaedic unit. The Consultant was from Europe. My Consultant asked me to perform on a middle-aged lady with a recurrence of a tumour in the right thigh. He told me to take the right leg off from the hip joint down to the toes. I did as advised. Two days afterwards, I was in theatre. I got a phone call and my Consultant was asking me whether on the leg which I had removed, had I seen any tumour. I said, "You told me to take the leg off. I did what you said. You did not tell me to do any dissection to look for a tumour. I did the operation myself with Junior Arabic Doctor assistant."

Obviously, it was a very big mistake, my Consultant said on the phone. The pathologist could not find any tumour in the removed right lower limb. I said nothing. My Consultant took full responsibility with no fault to me nor my Assistant Surgeon. The matter reached to main hospital Administrator. Nothing happened to him. When I left the hospital on my own, my Consultant was still working in the Department. Everybody knows that this was very big mistake.

But, believe me, in my career of Orthopaedics, now that I am retired, I can say I have seen worse than this. Every day we come to know about incidents like these from the media, either newspapers or TV news or other sources. Like the work I heard only a few days ago, whilst I am writing this book. I heard on the news on TV that two doctors of one of the well-known hospitals were suspended because they declared a new born dead when the child was alive. The parents came to know while taking the child, declared dead, back home. They got the child admitted. I am going to be seventy years old and never in my medical career had I heard something like this. I am, as I have written, been involved in doing ward rounds with VIP Consultants when the patient was already dead and the above case of a removal of a whole lower limb with no tumour.

I have mentioned these complications in my career but every day in the newspapers, doctors are being sued due to negligence or a mistake. I fully agree that mistakes happen. But I can assure you that the good thing done by doctors weighs far more than these mistakes. I have not seen any doctor doing any mistake deliberately. Especially these days with so much supervision. The room for mistakes to occur is small but it does happen. However on the majority of the jobs done, wherever I have worked, has been very good and done for mankind. All the medical staff contribute to this good work.

I personally feel the top job is done by nurses. I know the result comes from collective efforts from people who are all are very good, but the nurses are outstanding.

The second incident I remember is when I joined my job whilst at the airport on my first arrival in Riyadh from London. I thought my job was for one year but my intuition told me that I would stay here for twelve years. Now, after twelve years, I had a very good life in Saudi Arabia. I resigned, the reason being the education of my children. When the children are above age of fourteen years, there are no facilities like that of an English school. The only option is to send the children to boarding school and keep doing my job in Saudi Arabia. I opted to resign for my children's education. I went to Saudi only for my children. I resigned because of my children, so that they have a proper education.

In my department all the Consultants and the other staff were surprised of my decision. My Chief of Orthopaedics called me to stay and send my children to boarding school. They sent my friend and colleague to convince me. But I said there is no point even if you pay me more. I have done so much hard work only for my children and I am not going to spoil everything. Eventually, everybody realised that I am not wrong to do what I had opted to do. Now, at this age, now in London, my colleagues who were in Saudi Arabia tell me I took the best decision and stuck to it and they tell me, 'See what you have achieved.' My Son is going to be a Consultant in three or four years and my daughter is a banker at the age of twenty-six. I also believe everybody needs financial help, but I believe my biggest achievement is the outcome of my children in their fields, which is well recognised by everyone.

My first life was when I became aware of my existence on this beautiful planet Earth. My second life was when I became a doctor to start my medical career. My third life was the beginning of London life. The fourth and most important was starting family life. My fifth start of life was my new one in Saudi Arabia. Now the sixth one was to start life as a locum doctor in the UK. Until now, I thoroughly enjoyed every life, every bit of it. I did a local job in the UK. As a Junior Doctor, registrar, staff grade and Consultant. Every job was important to me, like my job in Saudi Arabia. Sometimes, without mistakes, the hospital staff get concerned, which meant I had to look for another job. I don't know what my mistake was, but the staff were concerned. What can you do? Nothing. Good luck to me and good luck to them. I was very lucky to get jobs regularly and I hardly remember when I had to rest for any prolonged period of time.

The best job of mine, I remember, are the jobs of Consultant Orthopaedics in Grimsby and the Trauma Centre in Birmingham. I started as a locum for one month. Every month my job was extended by up to six months. After six months they called and told me that they are very pleased with my job and the hospital administration wished to extend my job but because of a finance problem, I had to join their NHS Service because the financial issues may continue for few more months to a year or more. After consulting my family, I took up the new job. I continued my work without any tension or worry. I have got used to doing private jobs. This hospital administration was quite impressed by my work. As the time passed, my administration approached me asking me to work in another sister hospital of Grimsby. I took up the job. Now I was working in two hospitals. My Consultant colleagues got concerned. One of the Consultants spoke to me about this. I explained to him that I have two children, a boy and a girl, both in boarding school. One is going to be a doctor and other, my daughter, is looking to become a banker in London. The Consultant asking me was convinced because his son was also going to become a doctor studying at that time.

He told me it was alright that I could carry on working in two hospitals. He said he would speak to other Consultants. The main reason given by my administration was that they wanted me to bring the theatre list down, which I did very well. No doubt, at the end of the day, I used to feel so tired that I just had something to eat, went to bed in order to start again the next day. Eventually, after three years, a permanent Consultant got appointed and I left Grimsby. But after six months, I was called to the job again. Whenever the administration persons used to come to theatre, my juniors used to look for me and say "Your administration people are looking for you." They only wanted me to do extra theatre lists. I don't remember how many extra theatre lists I did. No doubt, I made lots of money. Looking at our bank balance, once my wife asked if everything was alright. I said, don't worry, let the money come, we are not doing anything wrong. It is our hard-earned money. This money was only from doing so much extra theatre lists. It seemed to me as if I was always in theatre.

My best job was as a Consultant in trauma at the Birmingham Hospital Trauma Centre. The patients were military personnel who were injured. They used to come for treatment from Afghanistan. In my life, I had never seen these types of injuries. Young soldiers would come to the Trauma Centre with horrible injuries which were scary to look at. I remember one of the theatre sisters saying to the others, "Do we have to treat these injuries?" Another theatre sister replied, "Someone has to deal with them. It is not only the treatment but what about after the treatment? The young man has his whole life in front of him." Who has got the answer? I don't know. My work was highly appreciated and my job was extended there that too as a private locum Consultant. This unit had a Senior Trauma Surgeon and Professor as well.

That was the best job of my life. It was very tough and demanding dealing with the trauma cases.

I kept doing my locum job until I joined another hospital in the UK. I did the job for ten days and then the administration asked me to leave because of staff concern. The Consultant in charge of the Orthopaedic Department did not operate himself but assisted his

Junior in minor operations. In those ten days, I did thirty-four cases of hips and knee replacements along with other operations. The regular Consultant did just one. I complained to the hospital and exposed the Consultant in charge. He was a regular NHS Consultant and the Head of the Department, and he was making a fool of such a remarkable NHS service. I complained that this Consultant only wanted to do private cases. He did not want to bring down the NHS theatre list. His thinking was the other way around, not to work but to get the whole Consultant NHS salary and at the same time do private surgery. The matter got referred to the NHS. I had to answer the inquiry, because I did the job of the whistle blower. I went to Manchester with my lawyer as I was protected by the Medical Defence Union. I knew about these types of hearings as I had attended an inquiry in India thirty-five years ago, but this one was different as I had to attend in front of the inquiry committee in UK. It was the same type of scene at the inquiry. We were in a big boardroom with a round table but there were a lot of NHS personnel sitting around the table with secretaries to record the proceedings in the room. I, with the lawyer, went in when they called for us to come in. I was not supposed to say anything apart from my name and my GMC number. I did as I was advised by my lawyer. My lawyer did the rest of talking, although at times he had to ask me things when he did not know the answer to the question.

The verdict at the end of the meeting was that I could continue doing NHS work but under supervision. I did not know what happened to the Consultant I complained about but I was not interested. I did not want to know and I still have no idea what happened to him. My duty was to inform about any wrong doing by the NHS Consultants. This is because the Consultants' NHS theatre lists did not come down. Unless this is sorted out, the theatre list number would never come down. I am glad I complained. My wife said, because she typed the complaint, "Are you sure you want to do this, a whistle-blower's future can be tough". I said that I was reaching my retirement age and that I had done my job sincerely. "Let me do this last act. At least someone is there to tell NHS that the Consultant theatre list is not coming down. It's because of my sacrifice that things may improve, God will bless me."

I continued my job doing as a locum surgeon but I was finding it difficult working under supervision because the doctor who supervised me was not happy and usually embarrassed, or used to take it as a formality. This tussle was getting worse. It seems as if they had difficulty in coping. I understood that the Doctor who was junior to me in all aspects would find it difficult to supervise me. Because of this mental struggle, I started drinking more which then started affecting my family. My wife and my GP friend suggested I go to my GP and get some help. I did not want to go but they pushed me. The GP, instead of helping me, referred the case to GMC and stated that I was drinking more alcohol than required. Again, I had to attend an inquiry held by the GMC. It was held in the same board room with the GMC staff members around table, myself and my lawyer. This time, because I went to the GP, on my own for help, the complaint by the GP was over-ruled and I was allowed to work but again under supervision.

I got fed up with these actions which started when I complained about the regular Consultant not doing his job properly and getting NHS money without doing work. In the meantime, my family relations with my wife deteriorated and my drinking got worse. I did not like it. I thought about it and I got the answer by myself. I said, "No point continuing like this, this will lead to more drinking which I do not want to do." I said to myself, enough is enough. I decided myself to leave the NHS job and go to India and do charity work as a Consultant in one of the charitable hospitals. I had almost reached my retirement age and there was no point in unnecessary suffering. I now think I feel my decision was very right, otherwise the deterioration of my heath in England because of my drinking would have caused damage to me.

In India, I started my new life, number seven, at my age of retirement. I was working in three of the hospitals in India.

I had lived in the UK for more than thirty years and it became very difficult to live in India because of the hygiene and heat problems. I got admitted in hospital twice because of these two factors. It got worse in the Summer when temperature would rise above forty-five degrees, it was as if I was living in Saudi Arabia. All of my neighbours in India and my staff members in the hospital advised me to go back to UK because I was not adjusting there. The heat and hygiene there would kill me and I was living in a rented flat spending money unnecessarily. There was no point working in the hospital. My friends, neighbours and relatives in India would say, "What is the point in carrying on in this condition which will take your life away forever? They say the weather is going to get worse. Before any disaster happens, go back to the UK." At least my family and medical services there wouldn't allow me to die. I took their advice and came back to the UK.

I came back as advised by my hospital colleagues, relatives and neighbours. I think it was the right decision. It is quite common when the wife lives apart from the husband for a long time to become the dominant personality in the house. She gets used to it. When the husband suddenly starts living together with her again, her dominant nature which has become more prominent finds it difficult to adjust with another or with a dominant person like me. I started facing this difficultly because most of the time I was away working in the hospital, away from home. I used to coming home only on weekends when I was not working. My son, who is also a doctor, picked up on everything. He said, "Pa, these things will happen. This happens with all families. You are soft and sensitive, that is why you feel more upset. Try to control yourself, drink less, don't stop, but cut down and eat properly. Take your medicine regularly." I adopted this regime which he suggested when I came back from India after living there for nine months alone. My wife became more aggressive on my arrival. She called the police the next day with allegations. When the police arrived, she said that there was an argument. The police said, "What is this?" I had an argument with my wife in the morning, does that mean she should call police? I asked policeman why they came. He said, "We have to come to do our duty, what can we do?" He said, "I know how you feel because we have your full record of being a Consultant working in three countries without any convictions and being a member of the Royal College of Surgeons." He knew that I had so many awards for my work and my name was in the newspaper a number of times for my work. He took me to one side and said,

"If she misbehaves again, give her fifty percent of the property and chuck her out." They left saying to me, "Take care Doc, what can we do?" She called the police twice more for minor allegations again and they left me without any action to follow. They left again saying only that this was a family matter and to contact the agencies taking care of these things.

Despite any troubles which my wife and I went through, I was very strict regarding our children's education, that it should be a proper one. Because whatever I had achieved was due to my education. My family is much closer to me now than before, especially my son, who keeps ringing me and asking me if I need any help.

As they say, nobody changes, it is the surrounding people that change you, as in my case. I don't know whether it has worked for me, it is a blessing in disguise. I am going to be seventy years old soon. I live on my own with my wife in the same house. As for my children, my son, my daughter and her husband, they come to see me and are always invited whenever they feel they want to stay. I myself, I do what I feel like, drink whenever I want and I take care of myself for my food, health, hygiene and surroundings. In other words, I am a totally independent man free to do whatever I want, according to my wish. I will do what I want to do. I think I fully deserve this because I have worked so hard in my life. I have given to everybody, my family and my parental family. Me being youngest, even there I supported them financially whenever they asked me when I was working in Saudi Arabia.

My Achievements

1st Class 1st Delhi 1969 BSc
Royal College of Surgeons FRCS 1986
Acclaimed in newspapers four times in Saudi Arabia
Merit Certificate Saudi Government 1991

I had a high class life since I became a doctor. I have been to many countries on holiday and now I live in a posh area with a big house and garden. The most significant achievements are my wife, the one I wanted above all, my son who is going to be an Orthopaedic Consultant Surgeon and my daughter who is a banker in Central London. My wife is the one I wanted.

I achieved all this because of the gift of God, my faith in God, sincerity, honesty hard work and intelligence. I believe in a certain way of working: to plan the action beforehand then whilst doing it, focus only on one singular point, no left, right, up or down, only the bullseye. Most importantly, in order to progress don't leave anything behind after the action for anyone to find any fault in your work.

Of my achievements, the responsible factors are as follows:

Faith in God, myself, books, alcohol, gifts of God, my intuition and different advice from others.

The most important achievements are the ones nobody can take away, my degrees and awards.

As for advice, resolve all before both going to bed.

Don't disturb anyone and answer back if someone disturbs you.

Live within your means and when your time comes, go to your limits according to your means.

Alcohol is God's gift if used properly.

Prevention of paedophiles, serious killers and terrorists.

I believe the only prevention is by detecting the gene in the chromosome as soon as possible, maybe even at birth of the responsible offender. All methods currently used for prevention are fruitless.

Palmistry and astrology are very accurate but not 100%.

One has to live in society and avoid bad people.

God-given gifts, if used properly, leads one to become a legend. But if not used properly then it leads to disaster.

Gambling – some people learn this art as seen in poker players and even in casino players.

God-given memory, knowledge, intelligence, physical power can be improved if used properly from birth.

If body activities are abnormal, one can tell they have a problem and act accordingly.

A good doctor is one who knows about the patient when they first see them.

In the medical profession, a bad doctor should change profession. This is the same for other professions but the medical profession differs because other human beings are involved.

Family and children deserve all but with limits, as they should be dealt the plan they deserve.

Nature is God's gift, and anyone going against this will spell disaster.

Reap what you sow, with the results evident from birth.

Good deeds are always rewarded by God. Time and place also play a very important role.

Going after money results in good satisfaction for the one earning by sincere means. Enjoyment has no limit but is best used in limit. When financial success is achieved, don't go for greed.

Good deeds done get rewarded sooner or later.

Quality is inborn. This is God's gift - when we sow a number of seeds, one stands up.

Anger can be controlled with meditation. This and living alone could be a path to a Supernatural nature.

Bad habits and bad ideas can be controlled and overpowered by oneself.

Revenge or destruction is not the solution to anything.

There are good and bad people all around and the good outnumber the bad.

Good doctors far outnumber bad ones.

Your own decision is the best but there is no harm in listening to others.

Learning from others is good if it's from a good and proper teacher.

There is no comparison with self-made success.

Any punishments should equate to the crime done.

There is always another way to do it, so never give up.

Failure does not mean the end. You can try as many times until you reach your achievement.

To hurt someone or commit suicide is against nature and God.

Faith in God always produces good results.

There is no shame in asking for help, and it can always be returned.

Helping the weaker brings more rewards.

Overdoing for anyone is not good.

Normal sleep has a pattern for every day. If the pattern is disturbed, it is compensated by itself.

The limit of intake is indicated by the body itself.

Natural remedies of the ailments are there but the best result is from the one registered.

In medical science, things can keep changing all the time until they achieve perfection.

Starting with prayer when you wake up, before going to work and before sleeping, helps significantly.

Bad feelings can be controlled by oneself.

Important discoveries and inventions have and will come from more studies of fauna and flora.

Depression treatment is not self-harm, there is always another way. Find out if required. If not by yourself, help is always available.

Sexual acts are the best when all organs are acting in unison. All ladies are different in every aspect and this also includes sex.

To live, we don't need too many people, only to be liked by few.

Things done in a normal way is common but things done in a unique way means reward, if successful.

Winning small or big is winning the same. With any reward or achievement, enjoyment is registered.

Implanted objects in the body may show results at any time.

Abnormal things happen without warning.

The most enjoyable things are always small.

There is always another answer to any problem.

It is easy to learn from animals.

The best ideas come out in the morning.

The most satisfying thing is to help poor people.

Every wasted object can be used.

Little things can give more enjoyment than big achievements.

You can be decorated if you are sincere, hard-working and honest. It's only a question of time. If you're lucky it will be soon, otherwise you will have to wait.

If one has to fight, always fight for the stronger result to become a hero. If not, people will forget with time.

Always start and have a big goal, if possible.

There is always another way rather than crying for anything. Crying results in zero.

Maximum enjoyment is when achievements are done by oneself and you see it growing with time.

Stealing something gives enjoyment for a brief time, but is not good.

The best teacher is yourself, but the clever one learns from other's mistakes.

After sixty years of age, one feels like they need to sit in hospital all the time to remain completely fit. Service is at hand, that is why rich intelligent people have an average age of around ninety at present. When I was a child, anybody above sixty – young ones, growing boys – used to think there were only a few days left until their final destination. I never liked the events of birth and death. The answer is avoidance.

I hate to be one person in a big gathering.

My choice of company is decent, neat, clean, posh, decorative, beautiful and natural. That does not mean it requires much money. Good living in every aspect is my first choice.

Negativity is self-created.

Right is right, beautiful is beautiful.

There is no substitute for hard work.

Whenever you need money, nobody gives it to you, not even the bank. But if you have faith in God, He sends somebody to help. This happened to me twice in my life.

If I am given a choice to come back, I would request God to give me the same life.

I count a person as close to God if he gives away anything without hope of getting it back. I have met few of these people in my life.

Father and mother will always stand by you without any doubt, but other members of the family can change according to circumstances.

Some friends stand out more than family members but not the father and mother.

If God wants, it happens. Once I left thirty lakhs rupees in a hotel room in Dehradun in a bag on the table. When I came back, the whole cash was untouched by anyone, whilst the door was accidentally left open in a rush.

One can survive on water for seven days or more. The body can easily recover after being replenished.

Some people have more power to recover quickly. I am one of those.

Animals and children have the same behaviour and healing power. A small child's intelligence is the same as a dog's intelligence.

I have learnt doing one thing at a time is more productive.

Sometimes in Orthopaedics, patients are better with no treatment. But, myself a retired Senior Orthopaedics Consultant, am not recommending this.

Most of the crimes are done behind closed doors and under the table. Involving religion is often used as a weapon which they get away with, without being noticed for a long time as in so many cases.

All girls forced into an immoral profession are not bad. I have come across a few that are quite different.

The anger for revenge or to kill someone should be restricted. Time is the biggest healer. God will take care of the rest, as happened in my case.

If anything is achieved in the wrong way, the enjoyment is temporary and has to be paid back with interest.

They say beauty is internal but almost always, apart from in a few cases, people go for physical appearance.

When working hard, like before taking an examination, if the subject does not go to your head there is no point in holding back, just rest.

Try to sleep for some time even if it is for minutes. Once recovered, start again. I used to take the help of alcohol. So many times, I would drink just to sleep for some time.

Drugs like amphetamines keep one awake but it does impair the ability to retain knowledge if used for reading. I have tried a number of times.

A cocktail of alcohol or drugs or any combination does not produce good results and can lead to death. Overdose of anything such as food, drinks, drugs, medication or artificial therapy is no good.

To counter anybody's anger, eye contact can play a big role.

The antidote for alcohol and drugs is only temporary. I tried myself and reverted back soon afterwards.

Interference in personal marriage life should be stopped.

Between the husband and wife, minor arguments will happen because of things such as water falling on the floor. But major problems come when relatives get involved.

Intelligence means one does the act but wins to one's advantage. However if this is obvious this is not called intelligence but something else.

As our religion states, suicide is the worst thing on this earth. The soul of that person will never get peace until the allotted time to the person is complete.

Donations in any form according to our religion gets rewarded in some form.

Regular visits to holy places also gives back the dividend, as in my case in a good way.

In the end, life is simple, only we ourselves make it complicated. If the body is controlled, life sails by. Living does not require too much which we never learn from our forefathers. Demands can easily be controlled by our body if we want it to. Minor disagreements are just waste of time. Major ones are always due to external factors and require quick action and avoidance. Nip it in the bud and there will be no chance for it to progress.

I have mentioned everything I want to. As I said before, if I have to come back to this world again, I will pray to God to please give me the same life.

Thank you God, you have given me so much in this life. A special thanks goes to India, my place of birth. Also the UK for my education and to Saudi Arabia for giving me financial help for a life for my family which was above my expectations. Thank you all.

www.ingramcontent.com/pod-product-compliance
Lightning Source LLC
Chambersburg PA
CBHW031500040426
42444CB00007B/1152